Alzheimer's: A Caretaker's Journal

Alzheimer's:
A Caretaker's Journal

MARIE FOSTINO

SEABOARD PRESS

JAMES A. ROCK & COMPANY, PUBLISHERS

Alzheimer's: A Caretaker's Journal by Marie Fostino

SEABOARD PRESS

is an imprint of JAMES A. ROCK & CO., PUBLISHERS

Alzheimer's: A Caretaker's Journal copyright ©2007 by Marie Fostino

Special contents of this edition copyright ©2007 by Seaboard Press

All photos, with the exception of Joe Fostino's early U.S. Army images and
the Back Cover photo of the author were taken by Marie Fostino.
Photos copyright ©2007 Marie Fostino.
Back Cover photo of the author copyright ©2007 by Erik Fostino.

Address comments and inquiries to:
SEABOARD PRESS
9710 Traville Gateway Drive, #305
Rockville, MD 20850

E-mail:
jrock@rockpublishing.com   lrock@rockpublishing.com
Internet URL: www.rockpublishing.com

Trade Paperback ISBN: 978-1-59663-562-3

Library of Congress Control Number: 2007923789

Printed in the United States of America

First Edition: 2007

Dedicated to
my husband, Jim Fostino
and my children
Kristina, Jennifer
Erik, Jessica
Regina

Contents

*Army Days, Private First Class Joseph A. Fostino,
United States Army, was awarded the Bronze Star Medal
on August 24, 1962 for meritorous achievement in
ground combat against the enemy during WW II in the
European African Middle Eastern Theater of Operations.*

A Note About Joseph Fostino

Joseph A. Fostino was born on January 20, 1926 on the south side of Chicago. Except for his time in the Army, he lived there all his life. Like many youngsters who grew up during the Great Depression day, Joe only completed the tenth grade. Along with thousands of others like him, Joe became a soldier in the United States Army on 4 May 1944 shortly after his 18th birthday. He served in Europe and near the end of the conflict, just as he was poised to invade Berlin, the Russian army arrived and his unit was recalled to France. From there he was sent to San Francisco where his unit, along with thou-

Army Days: Joe as a young soldier. Joe served in both Europe as well as the Pacific theaters during World War II.

sands of other soldiers, spent two weeks of intensive training in preparation for a beach invasion of Japan. As he was traveling east by ship, the atomic bombs were dropped on Japan and World War II came to an end. Joe's unit went on to the Philippines where he learned his civilian trade, truck driving. He fought with the Eagles 86th Infantry Division, Black Hawks. Joe left the armed services on April 16, 1946.

On August 24, 1962, Private First Class Joseph A. Fostino, of the United States Army, was awarded the Bronze Star Medal for meritorious achievement in ground combat against the enemy during WW II in the European African Middle Eastern Theater of Operations. Joe never mentioned this honor to most of his friends and co-workers.

Joe married "Jean" (Virginia) Gaeta on May 19, 1948 and they had three children, Jimmy (1953), Janet (1956) and Joann (1959). Tragedy struck early for Joe and Jean when Janet was born severely handicapped. Janet was placed in a state institution at the age of twelve.

Joe's wife, Jean, passed away in the summer of 1999. Friends and relatives alike feel that the death of his wife marked the beginning of Joe's long battle with Alzheimer's disease.

Joe loved driving his big rig almost as much as he loved his family. He drove big rigs his entire working life, mostly for the Teamster's Local 705. He was a devoted husband, father and friend as well as a war hero. Joe will be sorely missed by all those whose lives touched his over the years. He leaves behind three children, six grandchildren and three great-grandchildren.

Army Days: Joe learned to drive a truck in the Phillipines. He served in the Eagles 86th Infantry Division, Black Hawks.

Joe took his new skill and applied it to civilian life back home. He drove for the Teamsters Local 705 for many years.

Happy days for Mom and Dad (Jean and Joe), probably late 40's.

A Note About the Author

Marie Fostino has been married for 33 years. She is a mother of five and a grandmother of four. Besides raising her five children, Marie has had many kinds of jobs over the years—she's worked in fast foods, as a beautician, as a Nurse's Aide in Nursing homes and as a professional photographer. She's also been a certified Paramedic for over nine years and currently works with private ambulance companies.

Marie has always enjoyed working with the elderly. When she was a beautician, many of her clients were seniors and she loved giving them a helping hand, even picking them up and driving them to the beauty shop when they were unable to come without assistance.

When she worked as a Nurse's Aide, everyone knew Marie's patients, because she carried lipstick, blush and a comb in her pocket so she could spruce up her patients before breakfast. It was this work that first introduced her to patients with dementia and Alzheimer's and the terrible effects these afflictions had on the elderly.

She was living in Oklahoma City and working as a beautician when the Murrah Building bombing occurred. She rushed down to the site to lend a helping hand, but was turned away because she had no medical credentials. Although she did volunteer work, helping with the site clean-up, she was determined to gain some medical training so that she would never be "turned away" again. So, with five children still at home, Marie began her quest to become a Paramedic. She spent two years going to night school, spending countless hours away from her family while studying feverishly.

Much of her ambulance experience involves working with the elderly in nursing homes, which Marie finds very personally satisfying.

Marie now lives in Arizona with her husband, Jimmy. Most of her children and grandchildren reside in the general area so she's delighted to be always near her family.

Joe, Marie, Jimmy and Jean (Virginia)
at the wedding, April 13, 1974.

Background to The Journal

Marie and her family were living in Maryland when Joe's wife, Jean, passed away in 1999. Shortly after her death, Joe's daughter, Joanne, moved in to live with him and keep him company. Joe and Joanne spent Christmas of 1999 with Marie and her family and no health problems were noticed by anyone at that time.

In October of 2000, Jimmy's job took the family to Decatur, Illinois. During the following summer, in 2000, Jimmy and Marie began to receive a series of distressed phone calls from Joanne about Joe's mental state and behavior. Joe misplaced flowers sent to Joanne from her boyfriend and used a hammer to remove the bedroom door from its hinges, making a mess of her bedroom. She was notified by the police that Joe had been involved in, and deliberately left, the scene of an automobile accident be-

Five generations in 1996:
(Standing) Joe and Jim;
Joe's mother, Yolanda; baby Adias;
and her mother, Jennifer

cause he didn't seem to understand what had happened. Joe's mental health continued to deteriorate alarmingly.

His increasingly fragile state was making life miserable for Joanne and finally, in the summer of 2002, she called to tell Marie and Jimmy that she planned on placing Joe in a Nursing Home for permanent care.

Jimmy and Marie discussed the situation and agreed that they should, and would, go to any length possible to prevent this. At this time they were living in Illinois, about three hours from Palos Heights from where Joe lived. They decided to quit their jobs, pull their youngest daughter out of high school, and move in with Joe to take care of him. Marie's *Journal* begins at this point.

Christmas in Maryland, 1999, the last year before Joe became ill.
Back: Regina, Jennifer, Jessica and Kristina
Front: Erik, Joe, Melissa, Joanne, Adias, Marie and Jim.
(Melissa is Joanne's daughter and Joe's grandchild.)

Fathers Day 2002, (l to r) Joanne (Jim's sister), Joe, Marie and Jim.

Because Marie found full-time employment first, Jimmy stayed at home with Joe. Later, when Jimmy found regular work, Marie dropped back to part-time work in order to care for Joe, who was increasingly unable to care for himself.

Fall of 2003 took the entire family, including Joe, to Goodyear, Arizona. There, Marie, Jimmy and his family cared for Joe until he finally passed away, in the comfort of home and surrounded by his loving family, on 13 June 2004.

Jim (around 15) and his Dad, Joe, c. 1970.

My Final Tribute and Tribulation
A Letter from Joe's Son

Dear Readers:

This book is an honest record of the day-to-day events and feelings of my loving wife, Marie, as she took care of my father. In hindsight, I regret that I did not do the same, so it truly amazes me that I've been blessed with this final opportunity to reveal my own innermost feelings through the words that follow — feelings that will, I hope, help enlighten those who read them.

When the time came that my wife and I realized that my sister Joanne could no longer take care of my father, we made our decision quickly. We both gave our employers two weeks notice and began making plans to move from Decatur to Palos Heights, Illinois to live with my father. Quitting our jobs (with no jobs lined up in the Chicago area), putting our house up for sale, and taking our youngest daughter, Regina, out of high school created an extremely stressful time for our entire family. But the future would soon prove just how stressful taking care of a loved one stricken with Alzheimer's could *really* be.

I don't believe I would serve you best by trying to recall now — years later — the day-to-day events of my family's journey with Alzheimer's. My wife has already done a wonderful job of doing just that. What I want to share with you is how I personally felt during, and now *after*, those trying times.

To many people the thought of quitting their jobs, selling their homes, taking their children out of school, and moving to another city — all in the interest of taking full-time care of a loved one who's been stricken with Alzheimer's — may seem like a very difficult decision to make. But, for my wife and me, we found this to be very easy.

We soon discovered, however, that that would be the only thing that *was* easy.

First, let me tell you a little bit about my relationship with my father. There was never a time when I thought my father didn't love me with his whole heart. I believe that he felt the same way about my love for him. He was a good father, a great husband, and a greater man. Yet, up until I was about 30-years-old, my father and I would always seem to find things to argue about. We never cursed at each other and we were never violent. As a matter of fact, I was probably 40 when I heard my father curse for the first time. But eventually the arguing began to subside and we became closer than we had ever been. He was always there for me and my family … always (as was my now-deceased mother — *Hi Mom!*).

But the disease — Alzheimer's — not only changes the mental behavior and personality of the one who is stricken. It can, and many times does, change the behavior of the caretaker(s) as well.

I'd like to share with you just how Alzheimer's affected me personally. I'm not going to beat around the bush or mince words. It is extremely difficult and embarrassing for me to write this and probably even more shocking and repulsive for you to read, but I'm afraid that if I don't reveal the sad and honest truth, you may not really understand just how powerful this disease is.

I'll give you an example. Someone who's in the later stages of Alzheimer's will ask you "What time is it?" and/or "What day is it?" Naturally, you answer him respectfully. He may ask you the same question again a few minutes later. Naturally, you will tell him again, respectfully. Then, maybe ten minutes later, he'll ask you the same question again. And once again you will answer him, respectfully. At this point you'll tell your-self that it is the disease that is making him ask again and again. Thirty minutes later he'll ask you the same question again. You, of course, will answer him again, respectfully.

Now you might say, "What's the big deal? All he's doing is asking a simple question. Sure, maybe he's asked several times, but hey, what the heck? That shouldn't be too hard to deal with."

Now try and picture this going on all day long.

Now, also try to picture him asking you, "Where's my house?" — just like he did when he asked "What time is it?" and "What day is it?"

Really, take a moment and try and picture what it would be like. Do you think it could possibly start getting on even the most patient person's nerves a bit ?

Now, imagine this going on day after day after day, month after month after month. Throw in, "Where's the bathroom?" and "Who are you?" and "Where's my money?" and "Who's stealing my money?" and "Where is my car … my phone … my dinner … etc."

You keep telling yourself that it's the disease making him do this.

He gets angry with you when you won't take him home (when he's already home). He tries running away because he wants to get to wherever he thinks his *real* home is. Then you have to go after him and try to find a way to get a grown man to come back with you. This is a grown man who does not *want* to come *back*. He will fight you. He will curse at you. He will scream at you.

And, he just might defecate on your kitchen floor because he couldn't find the bathroom in his own home.

I am ashamed to say that at times I was very mean to my father. I would curse at him, pinch him, pull him, push him, and treat him by far much worse than I have ever treated anyone else in this world. Anyone else. If my mother was alive then, and knew how I was treating my father, it would have broken her heart … absolutely broken her heart in two.

I was sitting next to my father when he died, the actual moment his soul left his body. It didn't take long for my shame to set in — not long at all. For days, weeks, and even months I would apologize many times a day to my father (and even my mother) and ask his forgiveness. I would cry each and every time. I was ashamed and horrified beyond words for my actions.

At some point, after he died, I came to feel that my father (and mother) had forgiven me. In reality, I believe, that's the point at which I actually started to forgive *myself.*

I finally began to realize that the disease had not only changed my father into someone I didn't know … it had

Jim and Joe around 1988 show another great catch.

changed *me* into someone I didn't know. Someone I didn't like. Someone I hated.

My mother use to tell me never to say I "hated" someone unless I could honestly picture that person lying "dead" in front of me — and it didn't bother me. And I can honestly say that I 'hated' the person I had become.

I don't want you to think I put the entire blame for my actions solely upon this wicked disease, because I don't. I know that I am totally responsible for my actions and that no person or thing can make me do what I don't want to do.

But I also know that, in the 50 years previous to these events, I never once mistreated my father and never once knowingly disrespected him.

So what does all this mean? Where does that leave us? I honestly don't know.

My purpose for writing this is to let you know, in as few words as possible, just what this devilish disease can do, not only to your loved one, but to you and your family as well. If you haven't already fully made the personal commitment to care for a loved one who is suffering from Alzheimer's, then I beg you to heed the words I've written here.

Of course, I'm not telling you to *refuse* this awesome responsibility. I am merely asking you to consider — with all the honesty you can muster — just how heavy a burden this task will be for you and for your family as well.

If you have already made this monumental commitment … then I hope my words have given you some insight, some solace, and possibly enough strength to forgive yourself if you ever become someone you hate.

Dad … I have always loved you with my whole heart. Always. And you were right … I am my own worst enemy …

Mom … you were my best friend until my wife Marie came along … and then both of you were my best friends equally. I loved you more than I think any son could love his Mom.

Marie … I *know* there is a God, because only He could create an angel such as you. Only He could know the impact you would have on my life. And I know that Jesus Christ was surely the Son of God, because I honestly see His goodness in you every day.

God … I thank you for truly blessing a wretched man like me.

Sincerely,
Jim Fostino
Fall 2007

The Fostino children with Grandpa in 1988.
Jessica, Jennifer, Kristina, and Erik.
Joe (Grandpa) is holding baby Regina on his lap.

A Note from Regina Fostino
the author's daughter and Joe's grandaughter

When I look back today, four years later, and see how differently I pictured life at age 16, I still wouldn't ask for events to be any different. Mine may not have been the typical 16-year-old experience that a teenager would volunteer for, but when life handed me ingredients, I made one zesty meal. That was not quite how I looked at it at the time, however.

In the summer of 2002, we were living in Mt. Zion, Illinois and had only been there for two years. That summer, we had to pick up and move to Palos Heights, three hours away, where my grandpa lived. As a sophomore that fall, this would be my second high school. It was already a drag to switch schools, as I'd done before, but *high school?* That made the move ten times worse.

I used to participate in school sports such as track, basketball, and softball, but when we moved, Joe became my extracurricular activity. I was, and still am, a social butterfly — you have to be if you've moved as much as I have. Otherwise you'd always be alone and never get to know anyone.

But Joe's illness made it even more difficult to have friends over or be able to go out. The sane part of both my and my mother's day was when we woke up at 5 a.m. to run 3 miles. Later on, however, she had to quit running with me and slept as much as she could with her crazy work schedule. We would still have our talks about school and work and of course, Joe.

As always, I received straight A's and won Student-of-the-Month award twice. I always loved art, but truly enjoyed studying with my amazing professor, Donna Hughes. I especially liked pointalism because it took such patience. I also liked my incredible Spanish professor, Mr. Andrews, who is possibly one of the most respectful and understanding professors I've ever had along with my adorable geometry professor, Miss Faragoi. She loved the Chicago White Sox just as much as I did and thought I was crazy because I loved to do "proofs." These teachers inspired me to continue to do well at school because they taught my three favorite classes that year. They were what I looked forward at school each day.

I would come home at 3:30 and walk straight to my room, close the door, turn on my music, sit at my desk and do homework. Every night I finish by 6 or 7. My mother and I would then take a 3-mile walk, come home and watch Lifetime television together. When my sister, Jessica, was back in town, the three of us would all take a trip into downtown Chicago and walk up and down Michigan Avenue, State Street and the Pier.

It was hard to make friends, I was embarrassed to have people come over and meet Joe at first. I then realized that they weren't perfect either, and that Joe used to be an amazing human being… so why be shy? If I came across as "look at his smile, he is just so cute", they would then, in return, come back with another comment like "and he was so nice and sweet" or "he kissed my hand and gave me a wink!" I had one friend who made that year as best as she possibly could. Heather was my gateway to freedom. I still cherish our friendship dearly because of her outlook on life as well.

It was then the first month or two of my Junior year, my father had picked up a job in good old Goodyear, Arizona. My grandpa's memory had really slipped to the point where he couldn't recognize his house anymore; that was our cue that we could leave. This would then be my third high school where I became good friends with one special professor right off the bat, my Algebra 2 professor Mr. Spencer. Him and I would talk about everything before class and during lunch sometimes regarding my situation with Joe. I confided in him and felt more of a friendship connection with him than any of the kids I went to school with, but that's always how I was. I didn't really make any friends in that school until my senior year, but by then, Joe had already passed away. I had a chemistry assignment my junior year, in which I chose to do an assignment about something I was fairly familiar on, Alzheimer's. My mother and I made a 15 minute video clip of Joe trying to put a 3 year old shapes puzzle together and other simple activities that he just couldn't do. Some kids in class laughed, but I of course sat in the back crying. That is when I knew I was different than others. That is when I found out that I had more compassion and patience than I ever knew possible for me to obtain, but I had it. I had grown up within those couple years than I ever thought imaginable. I assume my professors felt the same way; they could all tell I was so much more mature for a sixteen year old than compared to others.

It's important to have friends and people you confide in. It's not okay to be by yourself, especially when this is an emotionally difficult time for you. With all my siblings leaving within a month of each other, I grew to enjoy solitude, and being picky with friends and who I would devote time to, since I hardly had any of it at the time. That hasn't changed even now. According to Erikson's Adolescence Stages, my age was the perfect time for me to decide where I stand as a human being, and how I choose to mold my identity. I wouldn't have wanted my life, and all the lesson's I learned any other way.

—*Regina Fostino, Fall 2007*

Jessica, Regina and Joe in Goodyear, Arizona, March, 2004.

A Note from Jessica Fostino
the author's daughter and Joe's grandaughter

My name is Jessica Fostino. I am the daughter of Marie and granddaughter of Joe. I always remember my grandfather as a very happy man who loved God. I was always excited to visit with him when we could.

I moved back home after a year away for college. At that point I assisted my family in the care-taking of my grandfather who had Alzheimer's. Being 19 and put into such a situation is very hard emotionally and physically. It was a time of sadness, regrets and sometimes loneliness. But throughout that time I grew more compassionate, responsible, and began to appreciate life more.

As difficult as that time was, it made me a better person. And I know my grandfather would have been very pleased to have known that. This has sparked an interest in helping others, whether they have this particular disease or another type of disease.

I know now that I am ready for any challenge. I love you grandpa!!

—Jessica Fostino, Fall 2007

Introduction

We all start out as infants in this world, depending on someone to nurture, love, and take care of us. We go through the discovery of everything being new, fresh, and exciting. Then the adolescent years come upon us and, as we become young adults, we learn different kinds of lessons about life from the people around us. Next, some of us go onto school while others find love, marry, and have children. Then there are those who find a career. Time goes on and we get older, as do our mothers, fathers, brothers, and sisters.

One day you look in the mirror and you are twenty-years old. The next time you notice, you're thirty, forty, and the years march by. You can't figure out where the time has gone. We've all been busy with our lives doing such different things; however, there's one thing we all have in common. Our parents are getting older. One day we may find ourselves expected to take care of them.

We know that, as we get older, we may lose our memory, sight, and hearing. But nothing can prepare us for what happens when our loved one's dementia turns into Alzheimer's. The caretaker inevitably feels lost and alone. Our loved ones are not themselves anymore—at least not the way we remember them. They don't know who we are and they don't know where they are.

Some of us listen to what the doctor says and put them in the hands of professionals in a care center for the elderly. But some of us take on the challenge of caring directly for our parents, just as they once took care of us. We're not sure what is on the road ahead, but we know that we love our parents and want only the best for them.

This is such a tale—a story of a tough love. I have worked in nursing homes and in the Emergency Medical System (EMS) taking the elderly back and forth between hospitals and nursing homes. When it was discovered that my father-in-law was not himself and his mental health was deteriorating, my sister-in-law found she could no longer care for him.

My husband and I discussed the situation and decided that we owed it to this great man, who taught us so much throughout our lives, to care for him in his time of need.

It was hard to deal with the man he had become. We had to remember that he was now a victim of the disease—that this person was no longer really *him* anymore. It was a greater challenge than we could have imagined, caring for him to his dying day; but it was also rewarding.

I wanted to write and share this journal in the hope that it might help others who are taking care of, or considering caring for, their aging parents. I wanted them to know that they are not alone. Don't feel that you've failed when you're aggravated, depressed, or angry. These emotions only show that you are human. Caretakers should value those days when they are blessed with the wonderful things their loved ones do. Caretakers must always remember the person they knew before the disease began to take its toll.

If you are just starting out, maybe this book will give you a better idea of what to expect.

I have found that running and enjoying a daily walk with God helped me get through terrible days and made them turn around. I hope you enjoy this book and that, in some way, it helps you to face and better analyze the difficult decisions ahead.

Over the years, I have dealt with all kinds of people, both young and old, yet nothing prepared me for the loss of a loved one to Alzheimer's. I had to jog each day and pray constantly to God to get me through those tough times. I believe that life is a gift from God and that none of us knows when our time will come to "go home" again. I do know that we are given many different hats to wear in our lifetime and that we're assigned many different jobs in order to serve as angels for God. I was given the opportunity to care for Dad in his time of need. Life is an adventure and I am not sure what God has in store for me next.

—Marie Fostino, *Fall 2007*

Teach us, good Lord, to serve Thee as Thou deservest:

To give and not to count the cost;

To fight and not to heed the wounds;

To toil and not to seek for rest;

To labour and not to ask for any reward

Save that of knowing that we do Thy will.

   —St. Ignatius Loyola,
    Prayer for Generosity, 1548

*This photo of Joe was taken on Thanksgiving, 2001. Joe was
probably in the very early stages of Alzheimers.*

In Loving Memory of
Joseph Fostino

The Fostinos (l to r) Back: Kristina, Joe, Jean, Jimmy, Jennifer
Front: Erik, Jessica, Regina, Marie (the author), c. 1990

September 1, 2002

This Sunday morning my husband, Jimmy, my 15-year-old daughter, Gina, and I packed up a truck and drove to Dad's house in Palos Heights, IL. We both had to quit our jobs and Gina had to switch to a new high school going into her sophomore year. At the house, my sister-in-law was packing up and moving out. As we brought our belongings in the house, Dad watched us, but said nothing. Sometimes he would joke with us. We took out his fridge and put in ours. We ate and watched TV and then went to bed.

We learned right away that the sad part about Alzheimer's sufferers is not just the long-term, but also the short-term memory loss. The next morning I found Dad sitting in the living room on the couch. Our boxes were still all over the room.

He looked at me and said, "Hey lady, what are you doing with my stuff? I put my hard work and sweat into this place and now I see a truck in the driveway and my stuff in boxes."

I tried to explain to him that we didn't touch any of his stuff… that *we* were moving *in*. Jimmy even opened a couple of boxes to show him that the stuff was *ours*.

But Dad was confused and set on the idea that we were packing him up. I left to take a shower and Jimmy talked with him. Later, while I was in the kitchen, he called to me, "Hey lady! I need to talk to you." And then, with tears in his eyes he asked, "Are you still going to take me dancing?"

"Oh, yes," I said, "and I'll take you to see Aunt Yolanda and Aunt Ann once a week." Then he replied, "I don't care *what* you're doing here as long as we keep doing that."

It's hard to see a man who I admired and looked up to for so many years, who *took care of me* and my family in countless situations, appear so helpless and confused. But I'm so glad that I'm going to be able to return all he's done for us by trying to provide the quality of life that he deserves.

September 3, 2002

Stayed up till 3 a.m. Tuesday morning cleaning out dad's kitchen cabinets. Took his stuff out and put mine in. I gave my son and his wife Grandma's dishes, saucers, cups, creamer, sugar bowl, butter holder, and salt and pepper shakers. They all matched. I hope it means a lot to them.

Dad stayed up with me till 11:30 p.m. and got up at 6:00 a.m. He has been doing a lot of dozing off in his favorite chair. And he talks to me about people stealing his money.

Vitals: B/P 130/62, P 64, R 16

September 6, 2002

Today is Friday and Dad is pretty confused. We took him to the doctor yesterday at the VA clinic. He was real upset. He thought we were taking him to the hospital or some "home" and not bringing him back. Although he was very upset on the way to the clinic, he was fine at the doctor's office. He was told that he needs blood work done and a complete physical. When he took his pants off for the doctor we noted that his testicles are very red, swollen and tender-looking. I was told to give him 800mg of non-aspirin twice a day. His blood pressure was high, 188/90. Jimmy was pretty surprised at how Dad answered the questions for the doctor but still forgot simple things. How confused he is.

The doctor did sign a sheet of paper stating that Dad cannot take care of himself.

At 6:20 p.m. Dad complained of pain in left side of sternum. Says it feels like heartburn. No chin pain or left shoulder pain or arm pain. Gave him four non-aspirin and pizza for dinner.

September 8, 2002

I am watching Dad and he is so confused. Today we went shopping at Target and left Dad at home for about an hour and a half. When we came back we found Dad in the bathroom, the top of the toilet tank off and water and feces in the bathroom sink and on the bathroom floor. Dad was frustrated while telling us he was trying to fix the toilet.

Carefully, I cleaned the sink and toilet, and mopped up the floor. As Dad was watching me, I showed him that the toilet now works just fine.

September 10, 2002

Yesterday I told Dad my plan to take him to lunch with his sisters-in-law. First he wanted to shave, so Jimmy gave him shaving cream and a razor. He noticed that Dad was using the wrong side of the razor, so Jim showed him the right way to use it. Then I noticed a rash on Dad's face from shaving, so Jimmy went out to buy him an electric razor.

Dad seemed more confused than usual. He could not remember at all where we were going. He kept asking me over and over again and I kept repeating that we were going out to have lunch with Aunt Ann and Aunt Yolanda. We were caught in a traffic jam and he was a little impatient about the car not moving. He wanted me to drive on the shoulder of the road.

When we got to the restaurant, he let the ladies help walk him into the building. He did not talk much but he sure ate well. Lunch included soup, salad, turkey, and gravy, baked potatoes, and bread.

After lunch we went to the nursing home to see Aunt Betty. Again, Dad let Aunt Yolanda and Aunt Ann walk him in, holding onto each arm and the facility gave us a wheel chair to use. He gladly got into it and we went up to see Aunt Betty who was up in her wheelchair. We had about an hour visit and Dad kept falling asleep.

After the visit we dropped Ann and Yolanda off. Dad had tears in his eyes when we said good-bye. Later, as we were driving home, he hit the door of the car with his fist and said how it hurts his heart that he is not driving a truck anymore. After a little while in the car, however, he could no longer remember where we were or why we were in the car. I kept reminding him of who we saw and where we went.

I don't think Dad went to bed. At 11:00 p.m. I saw him sitting and sleeping on his chair and at 5:00 a.m. he was still there. I made his bed yesterday and it was not ruffled.

September 11, 2002

Today is Wednesday and I found Dad in the pantry looking through the spices. When I asked him what he was doing, he said he was looking for some "cold medicine." I told him that those were spices and he said "Yes." He kept trying to pick them up and read them and they kept falling to the ground. Finally, Jimmy figured out that that he was looking for some pain medicine.

September 12, 2002

This is Thursday and Dad had an appointment at the VA clinic for the blood tests. He argued a little bit and finally went into the bathroom to clean up. It was a much easier ride this time. On the trip he only mentioned once that he wasn't sure where he was going and if we were taking him away from his home. I think he is more comfortable now. He seems to understand that we are here to help him.

September 13, 2002

This Friday morning I heard Dad outside moving garbage cans around. Gina looked into the garage and asked, "Mom, what is Grandpa doing?"

He is so cute. I found him taking garbage from one can and putting it into another can. Also he was putting garbage in my recycle bins. Jimmy had been painting and left tape with wet paint on it in the garbage cans.

"Dad," I said, "you have paint on your hands."

"Oh," he replied, "that's O.K." I had to get a washrag and clean each one of his fingers and he stood there and just let me clean him up.

September 14, 2002

This Saturday morning started with me, Jim, and Gina having a conversation. Dad sat there listening to us. He was concentrating intently on Jim while he was talking. Dad would ask a question and move his hands, like he understood what we were saying. He was so serious, trying hard to join in our conversation. Gina and I just smiled, because Dad was so cute.

Jimmy got him a new razor and all he does is shave all day long. I asked Dad how he was doing, and he said "not too good."

"What's wrong?" I asked.

"Well," he said, "I can't find my razor."

"Maybe you were walking with it and left it somewhere," I suggested.

"Maybe," he agreed. "But I just want to shave." Since Jimmy got Dad his new razor, he shaves all day long, while sitting, rocking, or walking.

September 15, 2002

Sunday started with Dad in a bad mood. He is kind of crabby. He had to get ready for church. I gave him one-and-a-half hours and he still thought I was rushing him. They had a wheelchair waiting for us at the church. Dad seemed to enjoy the service. After church we went out to Country Kitchen for lunch. We met his sister and her kids. Dad complained and got snappy with me as we were going in the restaurant and finding our seats.

Funny thing, though—just as soon as he was waited on, he put on a happy face. He complained about leaving the restaurant and later, at home, asked where his medications were. He must have walked too much today and be in pain. I have to let his comments go because he really doesn't mean them. Dad seems a little more distracted, and confused and short-tempered today than usual.

September 18, 2002

Dad is watching TV, but not comprehending what is being said. We are watching a segment about a mother who is praying for her son and his future to be in tuned with God. But Dad was telling me that it was about education and being poor and not having enough money for a good education.

Later tonight, Dad was at the fridge and fell on the floor and hit the back of his head on the cabinet. He did not pass out and I felt no bruising or contusions. For some reason he took off the top of the new milk carton, while all along there was one already opened.

September 22, 2002

This Sunday is a beautiful day. We were lucky enough to spend a day in Chicago again. Took my father-in-law to the Lincoln Park Zoo. Admission is free but parking costs $9.00. I don't know if Dad ever took his children to the zoo.

We rented a wheelchair for a month so I brought it with us. It is so funny to hear him tell me that he is not going to use it, that he is going to walk, and then, just as I get him out of the car, he'll tell me to bring the chair closer.

It is so beautiful to see the city buildings outlining the zoo. They are rebuilding the area for the bears in the zoo so a lot of the bears were missing. Dad did pretty well. I can tell now that when he is real crabby, something is wrong. We were strolling around and, as we left the house at noon having had no lunch, he began to complain. He said that he cannot do this all day. "Lady, I hope you know what you are doing," and "We have to get back," and "This is too much for you."

I got us some lunch (burgers and pop) and he was in a better mood. I pushed him around some more and I got him interested in some of the animals. Then he had to go to the bathroom which was accomplished with the help of a nice stranger. Then I took him across Lake Shore Drive to the beach and wheeled him down the whole strip. It is so beautiful to hear the waves and feel the wind against your face. Dad said he had to go to the bathroom again and I reminded him that he just went.

At the end of our walk, we stopped at the lifeguard station (which looks like a big boat) and asked them where the bathrooms were. Unfortunately, they were locked up for the winter. So I walked Dad all the way down the strip and back to the car where he started complaining that he had better go to the bathroom now. We walked back to the zoo, only to discover that all the wheelchair-access bathrooms were closed except one that could only be accessed by walking downstairs.

Joe at Chicago's Lincoln Park Zoo, September 2002.

He was mad that I wouldn't let him walk down the stairs. He forgets that he can't do that. He began yelling at me and telling me that he fought for our country and can't even find a bathroom.

Every time he swore I told him I was going to wash out his mouth with soap. As I was trying to get him into the car he told me that I had better have something to go pee in. So I found a gentleman to push his chair to the wooded area and let him get relief. After that he was calm again and forgot that incident ever happened.

He seems more confused these days. I think he sees things that are not "there." I was watching him eat supper last night and he put a napkin over the food on half his plate. When he finished eating the first half, he kept scraping the plate, as though he were trying to get food off. I asked him what he was doing and he said "eating." I uncovered the other side to show him that he had food over here. He said he knew that but wanted to finish "this side" first—which was the empty side.

Jimmy and Gina went to Decatur for the weekend. I think it was good for Jimmy to get away. This is getting hard on him to watch his Dad like this, especially since I am working full-time right now and he is at home taking care of Dad.

The fight will start as I try to get my father-in-law ready for church. I take him to a Baptist Church every Sunday. He was brought up Catholic, but I never really saw him to go church. I think he enjoys it but he's so slow getting ready. He forgets why he is in the bathroom, for example. He was in there forever last night and three different times I went in to see if he needed any help. He told me he was fixing the switches because the lights were not working. When I showed him that they did work, he began to "fix" the faucet. I showed him that the faucet worked just fine. Then he took out a sanitary pad. I'm not sure *what* he thought it was. Alzheimer's is a strange disease.

Well, got to go and get Dad ready for church. Remember that life is a gift from God. Do obey His will and enjoy the life He gave you. And when feeling real down, pray and have Him hold you and help take your troubles away. If you really believe in Him, He will make you happy, but you have to trust Him, read His word, and remember it doesn't happen over-night. But with prayer, you can feel Him lighten your load.

September 25, 2002

I think it is really getting to Jimmy between being home and not working and staying with Dad. Dad hasn't any idea what we are talking about most of the time, but he puts in his two cents and Jimmy starts debating with him. Then Dad gets mad and says, "forget it" and shuts up. Jimmy is out of patience today. Dad let me cut his nails tonight.

September 29, 2002

Dad is pretty confused today. I wore him out yesterday by being downtown for seven hours and so he slept in this morning and didn't get up till 9:30 a.m. That is pretty late for him and I had to help him get going for church.

His routine is a cup of coffee in the morning and then a nap in his favorite chair. So I waited for him to drink and snooze and by 11:00 a.m. he was ready. I had clean clothes laid out on his bed. I noticed that he changed his shirt but not his pants. I looked all over his bedroom for his shoes but couldn't find them.

His carpet was wet by the side of his bed, and smelled of urine. And, as I put slippers on him (I gave up looking for the shoes), I smelt urine on his socks. I asked him why he didn't change his pants and he said he didn't see any. It was 11:15 a.m. and getting late, so we drove to church along with the smell of urine. I figured that God didn't care if he smelt a little and Dad seemed so thankful to be at church.

Now it is 3:00 p.m. and I have tried three times to get him to change his pants. He keeps saying he *has* and I continue to show him the dirt on his pants. Then he closes the bathroom door to change again.

I notice how his ankles are swelling. Between his ankles and feet is a thin line, like a rubber band holding his skin together where his socks stop.

Bless his heart, it is 3:45 p.m. and he still doesn't have his clean pants on yet. He keeps taking the stuff out of his pockets, or handing me his pants turned inside out, thinking that he has changed.

Finally, I held the clean pants outside the door and when he took off his dirty ones, I made him hand them to me. Then I passed him the clean ones. Bless his heart, I heard him say, "I've never changed into so many pairs of pants in one day before."

> *Cleaning and Scrubbing Can Wait till Tomorrow.*
> *'Cuz Babies Grow Up, We Learn to Our Sorrow.*
> *So Quiet down Cobwebs and Dust Go to Sleep.*
> *I'm Rocking My Baby, 'Cuz Babies Don't Keep.*

I think of this poem as I use a lot more patience and time with Dad.

You cannot be in a hurry with him.

October 2, 2002

Around 6:15 p.m., this Wednesday evening, I think Dad had a TIA (Transient ischemic attack). He first asked Jimmy when he was going home. Jim told him he was at home and Dad asked him where he was going to sleep. Jim told him in his bedroom at the end of the hall.

I carefully walked him to this room and he asked me if I had anything for him to wear. I brought out his pajamas and told him that I would help him put them on if he'd like. He told me "NO!"

I left the room and came back about 10 minutes later. He had on his pajama top and was just sitting and starring out into space. I called his name but got no response. I took his hands and asked him to squeeze but still got no response. His pupils were constricted and he just stared into space. As I was talking to him, all of a sudden, he made eye contact, smiled and said he didn't know what he was supposed to do. So I helped him put on his pajamas and tucked him into bed. I put on some music and kissed him goodnight. He smiled and said I was kind.

October 3, 2002

I have been writing everything down, just to keep track of how Dad is progressing. Jim isn't doing real well. Yesterday Dad told us that he wanted us to take him "home." He said he liked it here with us but he needs to check on his house. At first Jim was calm—talking to him, telling him that this *was* his house. But after a while, Jim began arguing. I tried to tell him just to agree with Dad. He admitted that, today, he has finally learned that he just has to agree—that he cannot change his Dad's mind or make him understand.

Dad was upset again today, because he wanted to go "home." So I took him for a ride in the car to show him "his" house. After we drove up the street, I asked him if anything was familiar. Dad said, "Yes, I live around here. Hey, my house is around here. Where are we going?"

I explained that he wanted to find his house so I was going to show him. He replied that he *knows* where he lives and never said such a thing. I pulled in the driveway and he said, "Yes, I live here and what do you want?"

He was still a little agitated and confused and upset—I think from last night's argument with Jim.

Then I told him we were going to the bank. He took a check stub from his pocket and said, "This is my check." I took it and had some fake money in my pocket waiting for him. Later, when the teller gave me the money, I handed him another handful of fake money—$300 worth.

I used to let him hold $300 of *real* money until he lost $100 of it along with his wallet. I did eventually find his wallet but I hid it from him because, bless his heart, he gets so confused. I am watching him zone out more often and waiting to see if he has a stroke. He does have a doctor's appointment on Tuesday and I can't wait to see what she says to do. He has gone down so far from the last time we saw him.

Anyway, I do a lot of praying because I have found, over the years, that this is the only way to survive and be happy, compassionate and still love life.

October 8, 2002

This Tuesday afternoon we took Dad to the doctor. Got the results of his blood tests. Cholesterol is remarkable and blood is remarkable. He needs more B-12, so I am going to have to give him a shot once a month for that. He has hypertension, so he is going to be on a new medication for high blood pressure. He needs an operation for his hernia. The doctor said it is getting dangerously large. After that he will need a CT scan for neurological assessment.

Jim will probably have to stay at the hospital with him because he is so confused. But first things first. The Doctor made it sound as if he doesn't get the surgery soon, he'll be going to the ER on an emergency run and probably not make it.

150lbs. 180/87B/P 80 Pulse

October 12, 2002

My son came to visit us today. This Saturday was a good day. Went to see *Spiderman* at the movies and went out to eat for lunch. After that I helped my Regina get ready for her homecoming dance.

During that time Dad was confused. He asked Jimmy what he (Dad) does at his job, what time he comes in and when does he get paid. Jimmy kept telling Dad that he doesn't work any more; he's is retired and gets a pension check every month. Dad would be quiet for a few moments and start again on the same questions. Jimmy got upset and finally told Dad he wasn't talking anymore.

At 11:00 p.m. everyone was sleeping and I was trying to get Dad to go to bed. He didn't want to go but finally gave in. When we got to his bedroom I told him to give me his clothes and that his pajamas were on his bed. He was already angry and was quite short with me. It was taking him a long time to get undressed. I kept checking on him which made him angrier. Finally he threw his clothes out the door wearing only his pajama top. I reminded him to put his pajama bottoms on.

Dad was making a lot of noise and Jimmy woke up and yelled at Dad through the bedroom door. Then he went into his bedroom and yelled at Dad again from his room. Finally Dad just got into bed and I put his sheets and blankets on him and kissed him goodnight. I told him that I was very sorry.

Poor Jim. He went to bed feeling very frustrated and mad at himself. I told him he had to have patience, that Dad doesn't know what he is doing. And Jimmy said that he hates this disease. He *is* trying but doesn't understand either.

October 19, 2002

Life has been very interesting since we moved in with Dad. Last night, around 12:30 a.m., I found Dad walking out of his room. I asked him what he was doing. I opened his bedroom door and found that he had his clothes, cards, razor, and other things packed up in boxes he found in his room. He'd also take a pair of slacks and tied up the legs at the cuffs. Then he'd stuffed them full of stuff. He said he was packing because it was time to go home and no one was watching his house. I took all the stuff off his bed and put him in it, with his clothes on. I took off his shoes and socks, covered him up, and he promptly fell asleep.

When I asked him about it in the morning, he didn't know what I was talking about. I showed him his room and he said he must have been just going through his stuff and that he was sorry if he made a mess.

I got so tickled at Jim, 'bless his heart,' as he talked to Dad about getting surgery. Jim was calm and slow and very patient. Dad and Jim had a good talk instead of another frustrating experience. Remember life is a gift and we need to make the best out of it. Every moment is special, it may be our last, so let it count.

130/70 B/P 72 pulse

October 23, 2002

Hey, this is just a venting note. Sometimes it is not easy taking care of someone with Alzheimer's. Today I started out by getting up at 5 a.m. and running a couple of miles with Gina, my 15-year-old daughter. I got Dad up and dressed and gave him his coffee. Then we started our trip to pick up the people we were spending the day with. Picked up my 80-year-old Aunt who doesn't know anyone and is lonely while her 80-year-old husband is busy working because he won't retire. Drove to Joliet, about 35 miles away, with Dad telling me how to drive because he was a truck driver all his life and I'm not going the right way. I picked up my other two aunts, ages 80 and 90, and waited for a couple of young people to show up, 60 and 43.

We went to the nursing home first, before lunch, to visit another aunt. Then we went to the restaurant, where my sister-in-law took over and ordered for my father-in-law. That hurt my feelings since I am Dad's main caretaker and I only work 36 hours a week now.

On the way home Dad complained that I was taking the *long way* home and, again, declared that I don't know where I am going.

When we get back, he tells me that his daughter lives with him but I can come in for a while if I'd like. Later I find him out in the garage without a coat on, complaining because the boxes are cluttering up the place and he has to fix it. *Right now.* I try to explain to him that Jimmy is in the middle of cleaning out the garage but Dad is snapping at me.

I'm not complaining, just venting. I will go running in a few minutes and I will feel better.

But this is a part of the disease that is so hard. He doesn't know who we are or what we are doing. He doesn't understand that you are doing for him because you want to and because you love him.

It's a lot harder on Jimmy because this is his father. But when Dad snaps at me when I'm trying to help, I have to remind myself that he *doesn't know* what he is saying or doing. Please don't take this letter wrong. I LOVE WHAT I AM DOING!! It is just hard sometimes and today was just one of those days.

I love watching my father-in-law. I'm easily hurt when someone wants to take over what I'm doing—as though I don't know what's best for him. And sometimes Dad can hurt me by complaining when I am doing something for him.

Will that stop me? NO!!! I plan on taking him out with the ladies in 2-3 weeks and do it again. Well, now you know I am far from perfect. Still have a lot to learn. Hope you don't think ill of me. Just being honest and venting. Going to go running now and I will feel better.

October 24, 2002

Well, let me tell you a little bit more about the disease. Yesterday evening, when I was feeling much better, Dad wanted to talk to me. He wanted me to find out who he should speak with because he was thinking about quitting his job and he also wants to know how much pension he'll get. Also, he wanted to know if I would like to have his job. He is offering it because the teamsters make good money and he knows I'm a good worker.

I told him that I don't want that job because I work on an ambulance and we are non-union. He said that was great! Again, he wanted to know if I wanted his job and repeated that I would be making good money, especially being with the teamsters. I was working on the computer and he wanted me to find out how much pension he'll draw because he knows how old he is and that it's time to retire.

This breaks my heart to hear him in speaking from another world like that, but I try to humor him and let him know that everything is all right.

Then, later that night, he asked me how work was today. I reminded him that we went out to lunch with the family and went to visit the nursing home. He couldn't remember and kept asking me if we were out with the teamsters or employees? I kept explaining that we were with his sisters-in-law.

He said he was "lost" and couldn't remember anything about the day. He even asked "if he had a good time?" He was upset and beginning to suspect that I was lying to him. He asked me to call a couple of people we spent the day with so he could ask *them*. I called the aunts and they talked to him. He cried on the phone because they told him the same thing I told him. No matter what we say, he still doesn't *remember.*

That is the real terrible part of the disease. Alzheimer's sufferers often don't remember what went on just hours earlier. Much of the time they are in another world.

I love him so much and hate to see him upset. It doesn't bother me that he doesn't remember. What bothers me is to see him so confused. Then he gets on himself and keeps apologizing.

I am so grateful that I'm able to give him the quality of life he deserves. Being at the nursing home again and seeing the people sitting in the hallways and rooms and not talking to each other and looking sad makes me glad that he lives here and I get to live with him. A couple of relatives at the wedding last Sunday asked if there wasn't a place where we could put him because of his condition? But after taking him to the nursing home yesterday, I didn't hear anymore about putting him anywhere. They said the place was so depressing.

Well this was just to enlighten you about his disease. He tries so hard but is easily confused and understandably frustrated.

October 30, 2002

Today is Wednesday—an uneventful day. First, the hardest thing was to get Dad ready to leave by 9:00 a.m. this morning. I had him take a bath last night, which was like pulling teeth. I tried to get him to understand that he was going to the doctor. This morning I reminded him that we were going to the doctor. He was upset because he said he needed a bath. When I reminded him that he took one last night, he didn't believe me. It took him an hour in the bathroom this morning to get ready.

Finally, when I got him in the car, the fight began. He said he is *not* seeing a doctor and we are *not* going to make him. He is not going anywhere, he does not hurt, he is fine, and everyone has to die from *something*. After a while Dad and Jimmy got into it, and I had to play referee, which I do not enjoy. Dad complained all the way downtown to the VA clinic in Chicago.

I finally got him in to see the doctor and we were told that the hernia was not life-threatening after all. However, Dad probably has a joint degeneration (or something like that) and he needs x-rays of his right leg and hip. It will take three months to get the x-rays through the VA. I have decided to take him to a doctor in Palos Heights, IL, and see if we can get these x-rays much sooner.

The VA Doctor did prescribe Dad a pain medication that cost $100 which none of the insurances that Dad has will pay for. Don't know what the future is yet for Dad. How sad is this system is for our elderly, especially our veterans, with the long waits and the high cost of medication.

November 5, 2002

Today is Tuesday—an eventful day. We got Dad to a doctor who actually *looked* at him. He didn't like the swelling of his ankles and let us get his right leg x-rayed immediately. Dad also got a flu shot and a pneumonia shot. On Wednesday, Dad will get another blood test and a tetanus shot; next week we will see a surgeon. His blood pressure was good.

Yes—today was a good day. The hard part will be on Wednesday. He will have to get a blood test and can't eat anything beforehand. I cannot let him have anything to eat or drink from midnight until the blood is drawn for his test. Life is a challenge.

Jimmy said that he had an interesting night after I went to work. He left Dad for about 15 minutes, in order to pick Gina up from school, and came back to a mess. Dad had turned on the stove and tried to heat up some spaghetti sauce in a glass bowl on the hot stove. Naturally, the bowl broke and glass and spaghetti sauce flew everywhere. Dad told Jimmy he didn't know how it happened, but Jimmy saw Dad trying to take the sauce with the broken glass in it and put it in the noodles.

Such a learning lesson today was.

November 6, 2002

Wednesday was a good day. Dad went in and had some blood work done. The hard part, of course, was not to let Dad eat or drink anything after midnight. It was kind of funny because we had to take the cookies, coffee, and pop and hide them in the living room.

Dad and I had a good talk. He can tell me his name and date of birth. He is not quite sure how old he is and has no idea who I am. He can tell me all his kid's names except Janet. He does not know that this is *his* house we are all living in.

He asked me if I had any photos. About four years ago I made up an album for Mom and Dad as a gift. I don't think they really looked at it much, though. But he enjoys looking at it today and keeps asking me who the people are in the pictures. We had a talk about his wife. He asked me where she was. He asked if she had left and I assured him that she had died. I told him they were very happy and spent many years in this house. He asks me all the time where he lives and where I live.

He says he does not know who he is. He was able to pick out his wife in most of the pictures and his kids sometimes. But he seemed to enjoy looking at the pictures. Jimmy put up signs all around Dad's chair. Although he will read them he is still very confused.

Dad still says he has to go home. He is worried about his money, as well. Jimmy took a picture of Dad with his checks and put the picture up on the wall. Now, when Dad asks about his money, Jimmy tells him to look at the pictures to see that he got his checks.

I hate to hear Dad say he can't do anything right or he is in the way.

November 12, 2002

As the disease progresses the afflicted person moves into a different world than the one in which he lives. Dad does not know that this is *his* home. He thinks he is still working and during the day he thinks he is "at work" and wants to know when he is going home.

I find that he doesn't like to be told what to do. He can sense approval and disapproval, just like a baby, when a new Mom is nervous. Sometimes the baby cries because he senses how upset Mom is.

If the caregiver is upset then the person who is affected with the disease will be too. He senses how I feel and acts accordingly. If I'm short with him, he can be short with me. He is constantly confused. For example, Dad asked me for a phone number in order to call his son but then doesn't understand that he lives here. He thinks I am a "Lady" who just works here.

In order to get him to take a bath, I cannot just tell him to do this because he gets mad. I have to fill up the bathtub and tell him it is his turn to take a bath and the water is in the tub and a special chair is there so he can be comfortable and put his clothes in the bathroom. He finally gets in but I have to keep the door open a crack. Sometimes he takes off some of his clothes and then puts water in the sink and washes himself. I have to tell him to get in the bathtub. Finally he gets all of his clothes off and gets on his special chair and washes up in the tub, all along complaining that he fought in two wars and should not be told what to do. Finally, an hour later, he gets out.

I put toothpaste on his toothbrush and I watch him start to brush his teeth. As he is leaving the bathroom he suddenly wants to know where his car is because he needs to go home. He asks, "Will his daughter come and get him?" because he lives with her now. Then he is praying to the Holy Father and Mother Mary to forgive him of his sins with each step down the hallway.

This is such a sad disease. Just minutes ago, he told me he needed phone numbers to call his family. He was holding his electric razor trying to figure out how to make a telephone call on it.

I have no regrets about taking care of him, but this is another hard lesson in life. Alzheimers is such a terrible disease. But I love that man and taking care of him. He is very slow now and I must have patience and not be in a hurry while with him.

November 13, 2002

This Wednesday Dad was even more confused than normal. He told me today that he needed the phone numbers for his family so that he can tell them where he is. I told him that he lives with his son. I asked him if he knew his son's name and he told me, "No." I told Dad that his son's name was Jimmy and he said,"Oh, is that right?"

He has no idea, now, that this is his home.

I left him for ten minutes to curl my hair and he knocked over the tall plant in the living room. There was black dirt all over the rug and I found him in the garage with dirt on the floor, from the plant, and black paint that he'd spilled on the garage floor.

He was mad because I washed his hands before going back in the house. Once we got inside, he told me *not* to vacuum the rug. When I did, he got mad because I wanted to vacuum it now instead of later. Then, after the vacuum was put away, he seemed to forget the whole incident—it was like nothing ever happened.

Tonight we went to an all-you-can-eat Chinese restaurant. Since Dad was in his wheelchair, I got his food for him. He was eating very slowly. We were having dessert and he still wasn't finished with his plate. I went and got him some hot apple pie and ice cream. He was almost finished so I moved his plate of food and put the dessert in front of him. He kept going for the plate of food instead of his dessert and then mixed it with his ice cream.

Gina asked him what he was doing. He said to remind him not to ask *her* along next time. He doesn't want anyone to tell him how and what to eat.

To walk is very painful these days, even with the pain pills. Dad says that we don't give him any pain pills, no matter how much we remind him that we do. He still has no idea who I am and I live with the name of "Lady."

He says that sometimes his daughter-in-law calls him and "Where is his daughter?" He needs to talk to his daughter because he lives with her. We remind him that his daughter moved out, that this is *his* house, but he just doesn't understand.

We have been giving him fake money since he loses his real money and he is not happy unless he has money on him. He was upset because he lost his fake money. Later, he found it and had me count it to make sure it was all there. This seems to be the most important thing to him right now.

I went for a walk and returned to find Dad making coffee. He took the old coffee from the pot and poured it in where the clean water goes. Then put the new coffee over the old, wet ones in the old wet paper. It is so sad to watch him getting more and more confused every day.

Remember life is such a gift and family is so important. Treat people, especially your family, the way you want to be treated. You should be nicer to your family than to your friends. And if you are a parent, remember that your kids will follow your actions more than your words.

November 17, 2002

What is it about waking up on a Sunday morning and seeing snow falling and the ground glistening and sparkling? It's the sort of scene that can only put you in a good mood. The ground is so white and beautiful. I love that God made seasons.

Joe helping us rake leaves, November 2002.

Yesterday, we raked up leaves in the front yard. Even Dad came out because he just couldn't stand watching us through the window. But he was like a little kid, as I kept putting his gloves back on his hands. He said he wanted to help but when Jimmy gave him a rake Dad would just laugh. When I took out my trusty camera he had fun posing for pictures.

Dad has an appointment with the surgeon tomorrow. I sure hope it is good news. I hate to see him in so much pain. I'm making him get ready for church right now. He's like a kid as he asks me what he has to do. He makes faces when I tell him he has to change his clothes, and shows a bit of attitude when told to brush his teeth. Sometimes he is so cute.

Anyway just a note to say have a nice day. Enjoy the gift of life today that God gave you. Enjoy the people you are with.

November 20, 2002

This Wednesday was a confusing day for Dad. First, to get Dad in the bathtub was like pulling teeth. He just doesn't understand that if he could *fight in two wars,* who am I to make him take a bath? Where was *I* when *he* was in WWII and why didn't I make him bathe then? And of course, Jim has little patience and yells at him when Dad is upset with me. I am having trouble handling that because when I tell Jimmy to stop he turns on me and it becomes even more unpleasant.

Anyway, a lady came today from the Adult Club which is a Daycare Center for adults. It was a real pleasant visit. Dad will start next week so I can get some sleep after work. He will go two days a week right now. I think it will be good for Dad to get away and be with adults like him. We hope he'll have some fun with other seniors. Maybe he'll think he's gone to work and will know that he lives here.

I called the doctor today and got the run around again. When I talked to him, he still didn't know that I'd had the x-rays taken. Then I had to wait for the doctor to call me back after he looked at the x-rays. He said that Dad's hip is flattened out, has very bad circulation and is collapsing. The inner side of his knee is bone to bone. He said that he'll have a specialist call but he thinks Dad will probably need a hip and maybe also a knee replacement. He said this is a common procedure for people of his age. So now I am waiting for new doctor to call. No wonder Dad was in so much pain.

Anyway, tonight Dad was really confused. He wanted to *go home* and no matter what I told him he just did not understand. Finally, I just put his coat on and we walked outside to the front of the house and looked at the mailbox. He saw his address and walked back into the house, thanking me for bringing him home. Of course, after being in here for a little while, he wanted to go back home again.

He keeps telling me he wants to call his kids and I keep telling him that he lives with his son. He doesn't understand, so finally I told him that I *talked* to his son who will be here shortly. Every five minutes we have this conversation. Finally it is time for dinner and he forgets all about it.

I took his blood pressure which was 150/94. His pulse was 68. I gave him his B-12 shot. Then he began to act like a little kid. He asked me, "What we are going to do?" but he doesn't know himself what he wants to do. While I am trying to write this, he took his glass of pop to the sink and broke it. Then he tried to get into the garage, which has a big first step far from the doorway, and I had to stop him because I'm afraid he'll fall and get hurt. He is like a two-year-old and I have to keep an eye on him all the time.

He keeps asking me the same questions over and over again. I may know all the Catholic prayers soon because I hear him pray as he takes each step.

Remember life is an adventure and we need to take it, enjoy it, learn from it, and to take care of each other. That is what life is all about. Not what we can do for ourselves, but what we can do for others.

November 28, 2002

This week has been an adventure. First, on Monday, Dad wanted me to take him home and demanded to know why he has to stay in jail. I asked him, "Why would he think he was in jail?" He replied that he must have done something wrong. He said he is not putting me down, but he has to go and find his people.

Tuesday, after I got off of work, I took Gina to school and Dad to the Daycare Center. On the way there he was real upset and wanted me to take him home. "Hey Lady," he said, "you are going to be upset with yourself! Wherever you are taking me, a cripple... well, what are the people going to think of you?"

I dropped him off and went home to get some sleep. I picked him up about four hours later and he was so happy to see me. The aides there said I must be "Lady." It seemed that Dad was worried about me and wondered why I wasn't with him and where did I go? They had to pretend to call me. They loved the idea of the fake money we give him to carry around.

Wednesday went fine and Dad seemed to know where he was, but today he was upset again. He said he "was not right" and wanted to go home. If I won't take him, he will walk. It took some time to get him to take a bath today and finally, although upset with me, he got in the bathtub. Then, what did he do? He locked the bathroom door. My son was here so I had him unscrew the door knob so I could get in.

Then we went through the usual routine. I took out his dirty clothes and left only the clean ones so he won't get them mixed up. He was very angry with me. He asked me why I didn't make him take a bath in the war and why I made him kill people and children? When I told him I wasn't even born he answered me like a child, saying, "Oh yeah. Good excuse."

Well now, I must do something so that he cannot lock the door. He doesn't know how to unlock it. It's dangerous because he could fall or something and I wouldn't be able to help him. This is a first for us.

I think it will be a good thing that he goes to Daycare tomorrow. It seems as though when he leaves the house he recognizes it when he returns.

I wanted to take him dancing last night, but didn't. Too much ice on the driveway and I was afraid he would slip and fall. We will have to wait.

In a couple of weeks, Dad gets his hip replacement. His surgery is scheduled for December 12 and he'll be in the hospital for three or four days. Palos Hospital is not too far away. I asked them who would watch him when I have to get Gina from school. They said they would put a vest on him to keep him in bed. I'm afraid to leave him by himself too long. He is so confused already, and will have no idea of what is happening in the hospital.

November 28, 2002

Happy Thanksgiving! Today began with Dad, sitting in the living room, telling us that we were on his couch. And this was *his* chair and that was *his* picture. We said, "Yes. This must be *your* home."

"Oh, yeah," he replied. We had a great meal with turkey, stuffing, manicotti, potatoes, broccoli and cheese, gravy and cranberries, and lots of desserts. Dad seemed to enjoy watching all of us talk and every once in a while he would join in.

Later on, when it got dark, he became upset and wanted to go home again. He asked me to call home and gave me his number. I dialed and gave him the phone so he could hear the busy signal. Jimmy told him that he *was at home* and they argued.

Joe's nephew, Johnny, has a lounge, so I told Dad we'd go dancing tonight. We fought a little when I wouldn't let him put on clothes that didn't match or stopped him from changing his shoes into a pair that hurt his feet. But we finally got out the door and on our way. At the lounge we saw Johnny and he paid for all the drinks. Of course, I only had soft drinks. Dad drinks Seven-Seven's, however, and they brought him one.

We had a good time with Dad's nieces, Colleen and his granddaughters Melissa and Gina. Dad wanted to dance. They were not playing swing music, which is what Dad dances to, and I was afraid of his hip. I talked Regina into dancing with us and each of us took his hands and walked him to the dance floor. We danced with him, there, without letting go of his hands. I think he was upset because he wanted to twirl us, but he would have fallen. The man has strong arms and would pull us and push us all over the dance floor. We must have danced four songs in a row before he wanted to sit down.

We were there for several hours and I let him have two drinks. He wanted more but I would remind him he had enough. He was in such a great mood.

December 1, 2002

Life is full of learning lessons. We must be open to learn and live. We are given tribulations, blessings, suffering, and we must figure out the difference and learn happiness, patience, and love in order to grow and be a better person.

I sort of knew this most of my life, but now it seems I am being tested much more severely than in the past.

I raised five children and have been in a marriage for almost 29 years. I have had to fight to be strong, been so poor that we had to live on pennies to buy milk, been moved away from family and friends great distances. I have known loneliness. I returned to school, late in life, and discovered that I was dyslexic. But no trial has tested me or taught such lessons as I am learning now.

I can use your prayers when I find myself being short-tempered when I know I should not be; when I become aggravated with my situation and should not be. I am discovering my shortcomings and learning to deal with them. I will be a better person for this trial.

I need to thank Julie for the poem "A Beautiful Prayer." It is so true. I cannot just pray for patience, or happiness, or sparing of pain, or to make my spirit grow. I have to do this myself from what God has given me while I'm on earth. But I can ask God to help me LOVE others as much as he does.

A BEAUTIFUL PRAYER

I asked God to take away my habit
God said, No.
It is not for me to take away, but for you to give up.

I asked God to make my handicapped child whole.
God said, No.
His spirit is whole, his body is only temporary.

I asked God to grant me patience.
God said, No.
Patience is a by-product of tribulations; it isn't
     granted, it is learned.

I asked God to give me happiness.
God said, No.
I give you blessings; Happiness is up to you.

I asked God to spare me pain.
God said, No.
Suffering draws you apart from worldly cares and
     brings you closer to me.

I asked God to make my spirit grow
God said, No.
You must grow on your own! But I will prune you
     to make you fruitful.

I asked God for all things that I might enjoy life.
God said, No.
I will give you life, so that you may enjoy all things.

I asked God to help me LOVE others, as much as
   he loves me.
God said… AHH, finally you have the idea.

December 3, 2002

Today is the first time Dad has shown physical violence. We got a call from the Daycare Center today because Dad was getting violent. They said he was arguing with everyone. Then, when he tried to stand up, an aide went to help him and Dad yelled, "Look! She's touching me! I need an attorney."

When I got there I asked him who I was but he could not tell me. I tried to put his coat on, but this made him angry and violent. He would not let me put his coat and tried to get out of his chair, yelling, "No, you are not taking me back to Germany. You are all Nazi's. You are all trying to kill me."

It took three of us to get him outside to the car (without his coat). At the car, Dad had his fists to me and a growl on his face. He threatened to kick me and started swearing. I hit his mouth and told him I was going to put soap in his mouth to clean it up. I asked, "Did he kiss his mother with that mouth?"

I told him how difficult he was being and finally we got him into the car. I lectured him, like a child, about his behavior. He fell asleep while driving home. I didn't talk to him much at home. I gave him his dinner and left. I tinted my hair and played on the computer—just kept my distance for a while.

December 5, 2002

Today is Thursday and I am seeing another side of the disease now. Dad gets angry, now. He puts his fists up and tries to kick me. He's tried to get out of the car while I'm driving, and hits the dashboard, *hard,* with his fists. He grabs anything he can get his hands on (like my cell phone) and throws it while I am driving. His language is very bad.

I think the pain from his hip is causing some of this behavior. I was giving him Celebrex for the pain, but the doctors want it out of his system before his hip operation. I am just to give him Tylenol now.

I am trying to learn to make him more comfortable and remember that we are here to take care of each other. I remember the saying, "Be an angel, practice random acts of kindness."

December 9, 2002

This Monday morning began with Dad yelling at 3:00 a.m. from his bedroom that he's, "O.K. and cleaning it up." I jumped out of bed to see what was wrong. It was obvious that he'd had an "accident." He propped a chair on his bedroom door to keep us out. Even outside the door, I smelled the wonderful aroma of his bowel movement. I asked him if I could help.

He was adamant, however, and said he'd clean it up himself. It was 3 a.m. and I was too tired to fight, so I went back to bed. Then, at 5 a.m., Dad leaves the bedroom and starts down the hall. I make him go back to bed and tuck him in but at 6 a.m. my daughter up and vomiting in the bathroom.

Finally, at 8:00, Dad is up. He is upset with me because I am going to make him take a bath. "You know," he said, "I took one yesterday and I fought two wars and I am a grownup!" Finally, I got him in the bathroom with clean clothes. I am waiting, but I don't hear him splashing in the bath water I drew for him. I look inside and he is standing by the bathroom sink with his head and neck full of soap. Of course, I told him he must get into the bathtub and he says that he is leaving because I am bothering him. I did manage to get his nasty clothes and sheets and put them in the washing machine.

I am not venting, just telling how the week is starting.

But with a smile on my face, I love taking care of this man. I wish he wouldn't get so upset with me, but I know he doesn't mean it.

December 10, 2002

Dad has surgery today. We took him to the hospital at 10 a.m. this Tuesday morning and by 1:15 he'd left for surgery. At 5:15 the doctor came out and said everything went well and we could see him in his room in about an hour. Can't wait.

We figure that his recovery will be hit and miss. Tonight he should be tired because of the narcotics. Tomorrow, when they start weaning him off, he'll be awake and the fight will begin. They want to keep him here for three or four days. They also want him to go to a nursing home for rehab. I don't think so—he can't even handle being in his own home for a day. How can he possibly handle a nursing home?

This is why we moved here—so that we could take care of him and he wouldn't be in a nursing home.

When Dad got out of recovery he was amazing. He began talking almost immediately. He's confused as always, telling the nurses that I'm his wife and my name is Joann. He also must have asked one million times, "Where was he?"

He wanted to get up and walk. We got him to eat what they called dinner, consisting of clear broth, tea, gelatin, and ice cream. I told the nurses I would stay to take care of Dad, but they told me to go home; that he was in good hands. I gave the nurses my phone number, just in case. I said I could be there in ten minutes.

Well, sure enough, I was not home two hours when the phone rang. Dad had ripped out his catheter, torn off his dressings and tried to pull out the drain port. And, of course, he tried getting out of bed. So there I was, with my trusty blanket, as I knew I'd have a long night ahead of me.

He did not sleep. He talked and chanted prayers and begged me to take the restraints off. He yelled and swore at me. He told me he was going to bite me or knock me down. The best one was he when he said he'd tell the teamsters what was going on, because "It was not right."

Sometimes he was mean and ugly and sometimes he was sweet. I'd say, "Hush, Dad. You are waking up the house."

He would say he was sorry and be quiet for 15 minutes. Then it would start again.

Well, all in all, it was a good day. Dad is alive and feisty and I still have the privilege of taking care of him.

December 13, 2002

Today is Friday and I am very tired. I think the nurses had very few patients so they kept bothering us. Every hour and a half they were in our room. They had to turn him, change the linens, wake him up to ask him if he had to go to the bathroom, or come by to see his roommate. They would come in laughing and having a good time while we were trying to sleep. I really needed to sleep since I have to work all night tonight. Dad is doing better, but he's even more confused than before.

He has no idea where he is and I don't think he recognizes his daughter or son. He seems very weak. He is supposed to come home on Saturday.

December 14, 2002

My husband, Jimmy, stayed with Dad yesterday and spent the night. I got off work at about 5 a.m. and went to the hospital. I was told that Dad was to be released by 9 a.m. and that the doctor wanted to talk to us. The doctor wants to put Dad in rehab. in a nursing home. I am fighting him about it because, although Dad can follow directions, he doesn't remember anything for more than five minutes ago. What good will a nursing home do but depress him and make him worse?

It is now 10 a.m. and the doctor is still not here and I am getting crabby. I just got off of a 13-hour, all-night shift and I want to go home and get some sleep. I went to the nurses' station and asked when the doctor is coming in but they could not tell me.

I explained that I was told he would be here at 9 o'clock. I had a lot to do, I worked all night and I was tired. They promised to page him. I gave them 15 minutes and went back to the desk. They said the doctor didn't answered the page.

Finally, I told them that I was taking Dad home now. I said I'd sign the papers saying I understood that this was against his doctor's orders. The nurses got very upset and called the supervisor. I went back to the room to get Dad dressed and a few minutes later the phone rang. It was one of his doctors, asking if I could wait about an hour for him to get there and release Dad. I told him I was leaving at 11:15, whether he showed up or not.

Finally, at 10:45, one of the doctors arrived and by 11:00 the other doctor showed up. Then the therapy people arrived and by the time we got all the paperwork done, it was noon before we were able to leave.

Dad was getting antsy and wanted out of there. We were not moving fast enough. When the P.T. people came in to help get him in his wheelchair, it seemed like it took him forever and all he did was argue. He wanted out and was very upset because we weren't moving fast enough.

I was told that Medicare was going to supply us with a walker and a raised commode. Someone from rehab will come by a couple of times a week and social services are supposed to come to see what we need. I am so glad that they are going to work with us.

December 15, 2002

Just got back from running 3 miles. I had no idea how stiff my legs got from living in the hospital last week. Even though I was working and kickboxing, I sat around more than usual. I woke up with aches on the right side of my body including my shoulder, arm, and leg. Now I think it must be from using the belt I put around Dad's waist to help him walk. I didn't know I used so much muscle to do this.

Now we have a monitor in Dad's room so we can hear him get up or move around. I heard him get up and ran into his room. I put on his pants and shoes for him, while he cried, because he insists that can do this himself.

I was told that Dad is not to lean down until his hip heals. Now he's telling me that there is a cut on the side of his hip and points it out. He keeps taking off the dressing and I keep putting it back on. I make him repeat after me, "My hip has to heal. My hip has to heal."

He has no clue that he was in the hospital last week, so I haven't taken off his white bracelets yet. This way I can prove to him that he was in the hospital and that is why his hip has to heal.

Now he wants to get up and I tell him he has to use his walker. Like a stubborn child, he puts his hands on his hips, and asks *why*. I repeat everything about his new hip and the doctor's orders. Then, surprisingly, he gets up, picks up the walker and walks pretty steadily down the hall. He is picking up the walker instead of rolling it and we pass the belt that I've been using to help him walk. He asks me, "What is this?"

I can't believe how well he is using the walker. Then he gets into his favorite chair and puts his hand on his head. He gets a very sad look and asks, "Where is my hair?"

Now this is bad. We can't find it. Dad is bald and wears a wig. Now Jimmy and Gina and I are searching the house for it and finally find it with his necklace and his rings. His eyes sparkled as he put on his wig, necklace and rings. I had to leave and cry some joyful tears to see him so happy.

December 17, 2002

I washed dishes this Tuesday morning when I got home from work and Dad was up. I took off my watch and hair band and put them on the sink. I took Gina to school and stopped at the grocery store on my way back. I must have been gone for about 30 minutes. Later, I noticed my watch was missing, I found my hair band on the sink but my watch was gone. I asked Dad if he saw it and of course he had no idea what I was talking about. When I put Dad to bed that night I and made him put on his p.j.'s. I felt something in his pockets and guess what it was? My watch!!!

December 19, 2002

Today began with me taking Gina to school. Dad was still in bed. This was very unusual for him. At 8 a.m. I finally went to get him up. I'm afraid that if I let him sleep too long he won't go to bed tonight.

He had his pajama bottoms and pants off. He wears special stockings to help the circulation in his legs. He removed one of these long, white stockings and had only the little bedspread on. He complained that he was cold. I do keep a heated blanket on him but he'd kicked it off. He claimed that the stocking hurt his legs and he didn't want to wear them.

I told him that he had to get up and he didn't like that. He said he hurt and was not getting up, so I had to make him. I dressed him, under protest, and he fought me all the way.

I told him that once he got some coffee, I could give him a pain pill. He just kept fighting me, telling me how I was hurting him. He hoped that some day I would feel the same pain. I hate this disease!!

Getting him to walk down the hallway was like pulling teeth and, suddenly, he claimed he could hardly walk. I had to put the strap on his waist and make him walk.

He maintained this crankiness. I gave him his coffee and a sweet roll and pain pills. My daughter, Jessica, was there and he continued to fight with us. I explained, again, that when he's like this, it's best to just leave the room.

Finally, the nurse came to draw blood and he told her about his pain and the stockings. She explained that needed to elevate his feet but, sensing that he was ignoring her, she simply told him he had to keep the stockings on. I've been trying to keep his feel elevated, but he doesn't like it.

While I left to take a bath, he managed to use his walker to go to the bathroom and back to his chair. But later, when we went out to eat, he claimed couldn't get up and walk. I had to pull him up and hold him up as we walked to the car.

After whining and fighting all morning and all the way to the restaurant, suddenly he was a *different* fellow. He was nice and polite and almost stopped complaining about the pain. He was pleasant all the way home. Now, I'm thinking that maybe the physical therapist worked him too hard yesterday.

Dad said that when he looks at me, sometimes he gets a little "tweet" in his heart. I asked him if has any chest pain but he says no. The nurse called and said his blood is too thin, so we need to alter his medication. His blood pressure has been fine lately but I have to watch for easy bruising or blood in his urine.

His blood is critically thin and that could be dangerous if he falls or injures himself.

I love life. What a learning lesson this is. Hopefully, when we learn something, we can pass it on to someone else. And hopefully it makes us a better person for it.

December 24, 2002

Christmas Eve started out rough this year. I had to go to the airport to pick up my daughter, her husband and their child. I told Dad that he had to go with us. He decided he was *not* going and told me so. I replied that him he didn't have a choice and made him get up.

Naturally, he didn't like that, and began yelling and screaming. He fell to the floor and refused to budge. When my son, Erik, grabbed his waist and I grabbed his legs. Dad got ahold of my hair and pulled. He was yelling and swearing and screaming, "Police."

Jessica and Gina tried to pull his hands off my hair, and with Erik's help we got Dad in the van. Meanwhile, he yelled more and more, "Call the police!" he cried while pounding on the window and dashboard.

The kids gave me a phone. I called his sister, to see if that would calm him down, but this only made him worse. The drive to the airport was a nightmare and took twice as long as it should have.

Christmas 2002 with the family in Illinois.
Back row (l to r): Arin Morris (Kristina's husband),
Kristina, author Marie, Jessica, Erik, and Joe
Front row: (l to r): Jennifer, Jimmy, Adias
(Jennifer's daughter), and Regina

Finally, after we picked up the family, he settled down.

Christmas Eve night, in the other hand, was great. We went to his sister's house for the evening. It was snowing, so it took two of us to walk Dad up to the house. His sister, Aunt Mary, sat next to Dad at the kitchen table the whole evening. It was sad to see Aunt Mary cry when Dad didn't know who she was.

December 28, 2002

Picture this, in a bedroom with an adjoining bath: music blasting, loud talking and five women in their underwear, ironing clothes, fixing each other's hair, gossiping, joking, laughing, putting on makeup and not letting any men in the room.

I suddenly realized how much I missed my family—the mess, the noise, the yelling, the hugging, the helping. What a way to start Christmas Eve.

Before I moved here in August, all my kids lived with me except my oldest daughter Kristina. Then my second daughter, Jennifer, and her daughter Adias, moved to Oklahoma. My son, Erik, stayed in Decatur to be with his girlfriend. My forth child, Jessica, moved to Virginia for college and my daughter, Regina (still in high school), moved with us. So the "empty nest" feeling was hard upon me. Having them all home for Christmas made me miss them even more and realize how precious they all are.

This was the slowest and most wonderful week of the year 2002.

We spent Christmas Day at home alone, if you call ten people in a house "alone." We went to the movies and saw *Lord of the Rings, The Two Towers.* The next day we went to the Museum of Science and Industry in Chicago. Of course Dad was with us and we all had a great time. I bathed him on the night before so he didn't have to take a bath that morning. It was hustle and bustle in the house with so many people and only two bathrooms!

I told Dad we were going for a ride and he was good with that. He went willingly into the car and seemed happy. At the museum we had a little wait before we were able to rent a wheelchair; Dad became impatient due to all the noise and crowds. But the kids were having a great time and once we got started, they took turns pushing his wheelchair. Each one would take time to talk to Dad, pointing things out for him or just saying, "I love you." He smiled each time they offered a little extra attention.

The museum had an area lined with Christmas trees from all over the world. We walked down that aisle and Dad kept telling us to, "Hurry now." But when we got to the section with the old-fashioned cars and fire engines, he seemed to calm down and enjoy himself. Before we left, we stopped at the old ice cream parlor for a treat. There was a long line, and Dad lost patience while we waited, but brightened up once he got his ice cream.

On the 27th of December we had an Open House. I thought this might be a good opportunity for Dad to see his family and some of his old friends. I'd discovered that many people were uncomfortable around Dad now, and they found many reasons not to stop by. I decided that an Open House, with Dad surrounded by his family, would make their visit a little less uncomfortable. These people all remembered Dad before he was sick and didn't want to see him in his current state. In any case, we all had a wonderful time. Dad even danced for everyone.

The next day the kids began to leave but that evening we went to a family reunion on my mother-in-law's side of the family. We had a great time.

My children are certainly getting an education on Alzheimer's. They have seen their Grandfather show the ugly side when he gets upset and acts like a child, fighting, kicking and swearing. But they also can see his nice side, when Dad tells them he loves them or asks them how they are doing. They are learning to be caregivers, not letting him get up without his walker or fetching him drinks when he asks. They have learned to be patient when he asked the same thing over and over again.

They can't believe how he doesn't sleep at night, as they hear me get up repeatedly and put him back to bed. They also had time to enjoy him. We did karaoke and, while Dad didn't sing, he did get up and dance. They made him a part of the family, just as if he always was like this from the beginning.

Remember, life is a gift from God, so please obey His will and enjoy His gift. Live each five minutes like it is your last.

The Museum of Science and Industry in Chicago, the aisle of
Christmas trees from around the world, Christmas 2002.
Back (l to r): Arin, Kristina, Jessica and Erik
Front (l to r): Dad, Jennifer, Adias, and Regina

SAD THINGS ABOUT ALZHEIMERS

He sits in a chair, confused, not sure what he is supposed to do.

When you come into a room, he says "Hi," just as though this is the first time he's ever seen you.

Sometimes he pretends that he knows you but you know it's an act …

He takes the phone and calls the same number over and over again.

He writes a phone number on a sheet of paper over and over again.

He is forever asking, "When can he go home?"

He forgets how to dial the phone.

He can no longer do simple tasks he's done all his life like make coffee.

He doesn't know the days of the week.

He doesn't know or recognize relatives.

He can still tell time, but gets a.m. and p.m. mixed up.

He still thinks he has a regular job.

He wants to know when he gets paid and when he can clock off for the night.

He repeats himself over and over again.

When you think he finally understands something, five minutes later you must start all over again.

He often wants to argue and refuses to listen.

December 29, 2002

Twice this week Dad has had an outbreak of violence. He's hit me, pulled my hair and tried to bite me. He talks so terrible to me when this happens that I am thinking of talking to the doctor for behavior medication in the evening. I know he doesn't know what he's doing, but it's very hard when I spend all my time caring for him and sparing him pain to then be treated like this.

I just hate this disease so much.

Tonight I hate myself because I was arguing with him while I was trying to put on his p.j.'s. I hit his mouth when he tried to bite me. Then, when he pushed me, I pushed him back and he fell to the floor. When I got Jimmy to help, Dad told him, "Look what she did to me."

I think I've figured out how to anticipate when he's about to get violent. He asks questions repeatedly, over and over, and does not listen to my answers. When I try to get his attention and answer his questions, this seems to set him off. I think I need to be aware of this and give him plenty of space when this happens.

Jimmy is afraid for me and threatening to put Dad in a nursing home. I really don't want that. I was reading some more on his disease and it says that sometimes Alzheimer's patients become violent if their regular routine has been disrupted.

Well, we've had ten people living here for five days. That would certainly disrupt his routine. When he wants to argue now, I usually go into another room and let him talk to himself and nothing happens. But tonight he just kept things going and, as I ignored his comments and walked with him to his room, he suddenly became someone else. He was hateful and angry.

I figure this is because he can't *remember* things and *hates* that he has to be helped all the time. I wish I could jump into his brain and see exactly what is going on so I can be more resourceful.

I really don't like medication, but I hate the anger more. I think he'll be much happier if he is not getting those hateful moods. Oh, well—he is sleeping peacefully now and will not remember any of this in the morning. As he moves out of stage 2 and goes into stage 3, I will have to be more creative.

December 30, 2002

Good morning and what a good day. Dad was such a pleasant and kind person when he got up today—telling me how much he loves me and thanks God for me. Ran his bath water and, as he took his bath, I managed to sneak his dirty clothes out of the bathroom and leave only clean ones. I got to do some kickboxing while Dad was bathing. Physical workout helps me cope.

I gave him his coffee and toast and then took a mile and a half walk. Today is a good day. But I hate this disease. He's so sweet one minute and so ugly the next. I'm trying to get ahold of the doctor so that when I think he might be anxious I can give him something to relax him before he gets violent. It is a relief that he has no recollection of what happened last night.

Well, I'll enjoy the day. I get to go to work tonight. I do enjoy my job and getting out twice a week for 12 hours is great.

January 1, 2003

I got home from work at 5:30 a.m. this Wednesday morning. Dad decided to get up at 6 a.m. I tried to get him back to sleep, but by 7:00 I was giving him his coffee and toast.

We went to the mall and Dad used his walker. I'm trying to tire him out. He did real well walking in the mall, and said hi to an elderly lady who looked at him. Even when we ate, he wanted Jimmy to say hi to an elderly woman sitting by him.

But then the witching hour came. He asks, "Where is he?" and "When can we go home?" and, "Will I call his home and will I call his kids?" He starts crying because he is lost. He won't listen to anything I tell him. In the car, on the way home, he kept asking where we were taking him. When we finally pulled into the driveway, he started praying, "Thank you Jesus for bringing me home."

Last night he kept trying to sneak out of bed. Every time, I would go into his room and put him back to bed. Finally he said, "I am so quiet, how do you hear me?" And I have noticed that he *is* getting quieter and quieter. He has no idea that I have a baby monitor on in his room so I can hear him if he gets into trouble. But even though he's sick, he is smart enough to figure out that he has to be quieter so I maybe can't hear him.

One minute he says he is going to run away and the next he asks me if I want to come live with him and that he will live with me always.

Make good choices. Help people. Smile and say hi to strangers. It takes one person at a time to make this into a happy world.

January 2, 2003

Good news! It's great how Dad can get in and out of the car now without my help since his hip surgery. And it is great to see him walk around the house, mall or anywhere else I bring him. He uses the walker without complaining of pain and praying with every step.

I don't think he remembers anything about his agonizing pain just a month ago. We brought him to the mall and made him walk miles yesterday. I would not let him take a nap and still he only slept three hours last night.

Today we saw the doctor and then he had physical therapy. I had him fold towels and vacuum the living room. He looks like he's getting tired, but I won't let him nap, because I want him to sleep tonight.

In the literature I read about Alzheimer's patients, it describes common behaviors called Sleeplessness and Sun downing. Patients experience periods of increased confusion, anxiety, agitation, and disorientation beginning at dusk and often continuing throughout the night. Their 'internal clock' suffers a biological mix-up between day and night and results in less need for sleep. I know now that I have to be more creative so I can try to get some sleep myself at night.

It's so nice watching him fold towels. It takes an hour to fill a basket. He concentrates so hard and still doesn't fold them very well, but it takes his mind off "wandering" for a while. Just a bit ago he was trying to call his daughter's house again and hoped that she'd answer. He still doesn't understand that he's in his *own* house and that his daughter does not live here. I've learned to avoid making him mad by just dialing the phone for him. It's sad to see him show me his razor and try to make a phone call on it or, worse, to watch him struggle when trying to dial the real phone.

I can't wait till it's warmer outside. Then, when he wants to wander, I can take him for walks and tire him out a little. I am hoping that if I walk him the same way all the time that, if he ever leaves the house, he'll go on the same path and come right back home.

January 5, 2003

I'm trying to teach Dad how to play Crazy 8's. We only follow the numbers and the shapes on the cards. He watches closely and studies the cards hard, but he forgets how to hold them and he even has trouble picking them up. He *does* recognize the numbers and shapes, though. Maybe if we play a little each day, that might help enhance his sight and recognition of objects.

Tonight I laughed harder than I have in a long time. Dad was trying to sleep and I was sitting at a chair next to him playing cards with my daughter and granddaughter. Every time Dad closed his eyes, I would grab his leg and shake it. He opened his eyes, startled at first, and then came up with a witty thing to explain why his eyes are closed. At one point, he said, "I closed my eyes to see if they were really closed." Dad was also laughing and in a really great mood.

January 7, 2003

Twilight time for the Alzheimer's patient often brings with it increased confusion. After 3 p.m. he really becomes someone else. He has no idea *who* he is or *where* he is. My father-in-law asks me to call his daughter because he hasn't seen her. When I do, he tells her that he is living with his daughter here on the farm.

Tonight was especially difficult. He kept asking, over and over again, "Where do I live?" and "What is the address?" and "Can I call my daughter, because my family has no idea where I am." I tried to distract him by playing a game of Crazy 8's. He's having trouble with the game now and can't always locate the numbers or pictures. He places the cards on the table, face up, since he can't seem to hold them. This helps me to help him play the game. When I ask him for a heart or a number 3 and he says he doesn't have one, I can tell him to keep checking till he finds it.

It is so sad when he tells me he is lost. You can't really have a conversation with him anymore. He does still seem to like to argue, so I just leave the room or change the subject. He's still usually pretty polite. He says "Thank you" and "God be with you," all the time. He also says, "I pray for you," and I have never known him to be a religious man. I'd never seen him pray until the pain started and now he still prays. His prayer goes, "Holy Father, Jesus Christ, Mother Mary, Son of God, Pray for us sinners at the hour of our death. Have mercy on us, oh Lord."

He was raised a Catholic and one of his sisters-in-law gave him a rosary. He loses it all the time and doesn't really know what to do with it. He loses lots of things, like combs and fake money, and his electric razors. There was a funny thing about the razor. When we moved here we knew he had an electric razor but he lost it, so we bought him another one. Now we hide one so that when he misplaces the other, he'll still have a razor.

One of his favorite things to do is shave all day while sitting in his chair. Today I found a third razor in his pants pocket. He also gets mixed up and sometimes thinks we are a "couple." During the day, he knows I am "Lady." But at night he lets me know I can tell him when it's time for bed. After I get his p.j.'s on him, he'll slip over and ask me to join him.

I just hate this disease. He is not the man I've known for the last 29 years.

Remember that life is a gift from God and we have no idea when it will be taken away. So, right now, while you have the chance, tell someone you love him, give someone a kiss and a hug, be an angel and practice random acts of kindness.

January 8, 2003

Let me explain what a night is like. Dad will get tired about 9 or 10 p.m. I'll walk with him to his bedroom and put on his p.j.'s. I tuck him in bed and tell him he has to stay in bed and he must go to sleep. I'd better try to sleep myself because in 2-3 hours he'll start getting up. Because he slept in his clothes in the army, it's hard for him to get used to wearing p.j.'s—at least that's what he tells me. I tuck the covers tightly so I can hear him, on the monitor, getting out of bed. I go to his room and tuck him back into bed. He doesn't know why he is up and comes up with lots of weird reasons. He apologizes for waking me up. This goes on all night. Sometimes it starts as fast as 15 minutes after he goes to bed. Finally, I'll just put on a robe and socks, grab a pillow. and lie on the end of his bed. I tell him that I'm watching and he better not get out of bed. As I lay there, napping, he'll finally start snoring. I silently sneak back to my room to try for another hour's sleep before he finally gets up again.

When morning finally comes, I either dress him or run the water for his bath. And of course it's coffee time, which is the favorite time of the day for Dad. It is weird how he needs so little sleep. On my job, I go to nursing homes and see patients walking around the halls in the middle of the night. But I won't let Dad do that. I think this just aggravates his internal clock about whether it's day or night.

January 9, 2003

Yesterday was a delightful memory. Jessica turned 19-years-old and I decided that we were going to have a little birthday celebration, so Jessica, Dad and I went out to lunch. This is one of Dad's favorite things to do—*eat.* I had whispered to the waitress that it was my daughter's birthday, so after we got our food, the crew came over and gave her a balloon, some ice cream and sang *Happy Birthday.* Dad really seemed to enjoy this. He was so charming. He flirted with the waitress and was so sincere and witty, you couldn't even tell he had Alzheimers. I did treasure this moment because by dusk, the bewitching hour came and Dad was lost again.

Dad and Jessica celebrate her birthday, January 8, 2003.

January 10, 2003

This is a strange disease. Sometimes I can't tell if my father-in-law *really* can't remember what I told him five minutes ago or if he's trying to pull the wool over my eyes. He is like a child, now, in many ways. When I tell him he can't do something because he might get hurt, he tries my patience and does it anyway. I have doubts about his memory loss because sometimes he'll look at me, Gina, or Jimmy and wink when he's doing something he is not supposed to do.

Today I'm trying to give him a nice day, but it is hard. I woke up in such a good mood and he put me in a bad one. When I brought him to Daycare, all he did was argue all the way to the door of the facility. But as soon as we got inside and someone said "Hi" to him, he put on a happy face like nothing was wrong. We went out to eat and he was fine. We came home to dance to the oldies and he had to try my patience again. I would only let him dance on the carpet, not on the floor, for fear he would slip and fall. Like a child, he crawled closer and closer to the floor until I had to tell him to move back on the carpet. Then he'd get angry and start an argument.

It's no use trying to talk to him. He'll go off on other subjects or complain that no one appreciates what a good person he is and how much we owe him. I'm trying to give him a good time but it is frustrating. Please pray for me that I won't give up and can keep working to be creative.

January 11, 2003

Today is Saturday and it has really been a hard week. Dad is almost impossible to live with now. He's very irritable, verbally abusive, angry, physically threatening, and seems to argue constantly. He's wet his pants three times this week at night and I've had to change his clothes in the middle of the night.

I thought I could deal with him without resorting to medication, but I was wrong.

Today he's angry because he wants to go home. Naturally, we keep telling him he *is* home. He was arguing and yelling. He threw the phone on the floor and broke it. We stopped talking to him. He was yelling about how he wants to go home so we told him, "Go ahead. Go home."

So he walked out of the house. Gina and I followed him in the car. He walked across 127th Street to the Catholic Church. He stopped a couple of cars and asked if they were going to Blue Island, IL. Then he went into the church, stayed for the service, and walked back home. It was very cold to walk but I followed him in the car and Gina stayed behind him as he crossed the street.

I am starting him on Risperdal today. I have never seen anyone so hard-headed. Is it the disease or him or both? Maybe it's the overwhelming responsibility of caring for a person with Alzheimer's, 24 hours a day. I don't believe I thought it would be so hard. I thought I had loads of patience but Dad has tested me. I've gotten angry and argued and then I'm so unhappy with myself. I don't like to live like this. This is the biggest challenge I have ever had.

I know God isn't giving me anything I can't handle. I know this is making me a stronger person. Life is a long learning lesson. Remember each day is a gift.

January 15, 2003

The Risperdal makes Dad a little easier to live with. He is sleeping better at night although he has accidents now every night. I think this is partly because he's trying to be quiet when he gets out of bed. He still can't figure out how I hear him. He so quiet now that it's getting harder to know when he's up. He'll have an accident on the carpet and then get back into bed.

The effects of the Risperdal are mixed. He's sleeping better at night, has more of an appetite, and doesn't seem as quick to be angered. But his incontinence is worsening at night.

His memory is definitely declining. I left him alone in the kitchen for five minutes and he opened the refrigerator and poured salad dressing in his coffee cup. When I returned he said he had to get some more to drink. When I took his cup to refill it I discovered the salad dressing.

Now I'll have to lock up the refrigerator so he won't get hurt. He has another doctor's appointment this Friday. We're hoping that the doctor will take away the walker. Most of our arguments revolve around use of the walker. He doesn't want to use it and isn't in pain anymore. He doesn't understand that he's still healing from his surgery about which, of course he remembers nothing at all.

January 19, 2003

I have discovered that, with Alzheimer's, his good *moments* are very important. Because he's not himself anymore (and never will be again) his brain has "shorted" out. Frequently, now, he can't remember from one minute to the next what he said, did, or was doing.

This is why *moments* are very important to both of us. These are times like when I'm getting Dad dressed in the morning and he's happy and smiling. He loves when I give him a toothbrush full of toothpaste or when I fill the tub with water for him to take a bath. He likes when I cut his toenails before I put on his shoes and socks. He especially loves his coffee in the morning and something sweet to eat with it. We have *moments* when we are in the car and I put on rock and roll and he dances to it while I play my air drums. Or when we play Crazy 8's and I try to keep his mind from wandering and he concentrates very hard on this simple game. I remind him over and over which card he is supposed to match. I think of how hard he concentrates on folding towels or helping me vacuum.

Sometimes he surprises me and prays before we eat. He still smiles at me, sometimes, and tells me he loves me, with the understanding that this is our little secret. I'm learning to cherish how he smiles when I take him for a ride to McDonalds or when we dance together.

Right now it seems that there are more troubled moments than happy ones. This is why I've learned to remember happy *moments* and why they mean a lot to me.

The best memories, of course, are the ones we shared when Joe was really Dad. He is not Dad now. He is lost in his head and has no idea what he is doing. It hurts to see this. But with God's help we'll get through this time of caring for him.

I hope to do a better job than what I am doing right now. But until now, I don't think I realized how important *moments* are. Remember each moment with your loved one is important. Never take those *moments* for granted.

January 21, 2003

This Tuesday started a little different. First, Dad got up at the crack of dawn and was real excited about getting dressed to go on the bus to Daycare. He'd put some clothes on, which I had to change because he was wearing a summer shirt in the middle of winter. Then he was excited about brushing his teeth and couldn't drink his coffee or eat his toast fast enough.

When the bus finally came and I got his coat and hat and gloves on him, he didn't even want to bother with the goodbye kiss I gave him. But 45 minutes later, the Daycare people called me and said Dad wasn't feeling well and wanted to come home. They wanted to know if they should drive him back home?

"NO!" I told them, I told them I was sure "He'd be fine." I got some sleep, looked on the computer for Alzheimer's sites and took a shower. They called again at 3:30, wanting to know if they should bring Dad home now. I told them I was on my way to get him. I got Dad and then picked up Gina. We went out for dinner before coming back and giving Jimmy a little break between work and Dad.

Tonight Dad did not ask to go home but he got antsy and started wandering around the house. When he's like this, I need to follow him so he doesn't get into any trouble or make a mess. He doesn'tt like me following him so he decided to brush his teeth. I gave him his toothbrush, full of toothpaste, and left him alone. When I returned, I found him cleaning the bathroom counter with face soap, using his fingers and toilet paper. I told him he needed to get out of the bathroom and he said he was "staining the counter top" and I was messing things up.

I turned off the bathroom light and he left and went into his bedroom. When I started getting him dressed for bed, he got real aggressive and began fighting me. He was pulling at his clothes, claiming they didn't "belong to him" and asking, "Why I was being so mean to him?"

He looked like he was going to punch me but he resisted and swore at me. I told him he was not a gentleman, using language like that. Then I told him that I loved him and that I was getting him ready for bed.

He then said he was going to call the police—he fought two world wars and did I realize that "he was a man?"

Finally, after I got him ready for bed, I had to stay in his room for 45 minutes before he fell asleep.

January 22, 2003

Dad is really in the wandering stage now. I have to keep a good eye on him so he doesn't get hurt or hide something important or mess something up that could cost money to fix. He really resents me following him around. I'm trying to be creative and keep him busy so he'll not wander so much but this is very time-consuming. I'm finding my life more than a little isolated and if it weren't for my husband and daughter I would probably go crazy myself. I have learned to slow my pace a lot for Dad which is hard for me.

Today he wanted to fix the furnace and washing machine, so I tried to keep him busy vacuuming and folding towels. When he began getting into this wandering stage, I decided to take him to the mall and make him walk the whole thing. This it was hard for me, however, because it took him an hour-and-a-half because he walks so slowly. When I could see he was getting tired, we ate lunch at the food court and then went back home. He should have been exhausted, but when we got home he continued to roam and get into things he shouldn't, so we went back to the mall again for some more walking. I'm thinking that I may have over-tired him because he got verbally abusive, angry, and almost violent.

I have to keep my eye on him all the time now and still he manages to get into things he shouldn't. I'm constantly telling my father-in-law what he *can* and *can't* do and he resents me for that. He waits now until I'm busy with something so that he can get into something he shouldn't. I think Dad is harder than a 2-year-old, only because he remembers things he used to do and wants to still do them.

January 23, 2003

It is a beautiful, sunny, and very cold day. I feel guilty today because I made arrangements for Dad to go to the Daycare five days a week for four hours each day. I finally came to the realization that I am not able to do this 24-7. I need help, a break of some kind and the Daycare Center seemed to understand, so I felt much better. Now I'm able to face Dad with different eyes, knowing that I'll have a four-hour break from caring for him.

I think that sounds selfish, but now I can actually be off-guard, relax, and even sleep if I want to. This is especially important now, since Dad still never sleeps through the night. I've been up since 2:30 a.m. with Dad and I'm really looking forward to taking a nap.

Also, they'll give him lunch. We'll see how this goes, since the "witching hour" for Dad is approaching. I'm hoping they won't call me, like before, and make me pick him up early.

January 26, 2003

Well, Dad's gone to te Daycare Center two days now. It was odd to see that the door was locked when I went to pick him up. An aide unlocked the door and told me she'd had two escapees today. That really hit home with me as Dad tries repeatedly to leave in search of his "home." Sometimes we let him go and follow him.

When I entered the establishment I found Dad sitting at a table, writing his name along with some gibberish. I asked him what he was doing and he said he was "taking inventory."

When another, older gentleman came over, he hit Dad on the shoulders and said, "Come on Joe. We have to fix the furnace now." Boy, did that hit a target! Dad *always* wants to do that sort of work at home. I told Dad I was there to pick him up but he said he couldn't leave just yet. So I asked one of the aides if he could leave.

She examined his paper and said "Good job, Joe! You can go home now. We'll see you on Monday." Dad smiled and said "Thanks."

Right now Dad is wandering all around the house. He seems to be really happy when I tell him he'll be going back to work on Monday. I can't get him to sit and watch the Super Bowl though.

Since I get a break most days, I can face him now with different eyes. I think he likes getting a break from *me* as well.

Remember that you make *choices* every day. Choose to be happy and show love to everyone. Choose to be positive, not negative. Remember that, with positive motivation, you'll have a great day.

January 28, 2003

I have planned a surprise party for Jimmy since he's turning 50. Jimmy's cousin owns a bar called "The Wild Olive" and he's letting me have a room there to use just for the party. It was not easy, with all I have to do with taking care of Dad, but the party was a great success. It was especially hard to get Dad dressed and out the door, since this event was at night.

After we got there and all the relatives and friends from work yelled "SURPRISE," Jimmy let me know that he guessed something was up.

It was still great to see everyone and have a night out! Dad actually seemed to enjoy himself. He walked around the room saying "Hi" to everyone, whether he knew the person or not. And, of course, he loved the food.

When the music was playing, Dad had me out on the dance floor doing the swing. It is hard to believe he is still so strong. He would just pull me and push me wherever he wanted. I was trying to follow his pattern while trying to make sure he didn't push or pull too hard and lose his balance. He was having a great time.

Life is good. Just take one day at a time.

Jimmy's Surprise Party, January 28, 2003.
L to R: Regina, Collene (Joe's niece), Jimmy, Ed (Nanci's husband),
Dad, Nanci (author's sister), Mary (Joe's sister), Lynn (friend), Bill
(Lynn's husband), Erik, Betsy (Erik's girlfriend).

February 2, 2003

It's been a nice week. I've had Dad at Daycare regularly now, four hours a day, five days a week. I can't believe the way this has relieved the *pressure* on me. Having this break in the middle of the day was such a *great* idea. It gives me a chance to recharge after the morning. I'm feeling better and I think *he* is also.

When I go to pick him up he's often waiting for me with his coat on. They tell me that he insists that his daughter is coming to get him or, sometimes, he insists that they call him a cab. They tell him "O.K.," and then he just waits quietly for someone to come.

We went to a support group last Thursday. I think it's a funny thing that the people in the group who are caring for loved ones with Alzheimer's don't seem to know much about the disease. Some of them have been caretaking much longer than we have but they don't seem to be very creative in their day-to-day coping. I think sharing ideas in our support group has helped them.

Let me share with you a paper they handed out called *Attitude.*

The longer I live, the more I realized the impact of *attitude* on life. Attitude, to me, is more important than facts. It is more important than the past, than education, than money, than circumstances, than failures, than successes, than what other people think or say or do. It is more important than appearance, giftedness or skill. It will make or break a company ... a church ... a home. The remarkable thing is that we

have a *choice* every day regarding the attitude we will
embrace for that day. We cannot *change* our past ...
we cannot *change* the fact that people will act in a
certain way. We cannot *change* the inevitable. The
only thing we can do is play on the one string we have
and that is our attitude ... I AM CONVINCED
THAT LIFE IS 10% WHAT HAPPENS TO ME
AND 90% HOW I REACT TO IT.

February 3, 2003

I went to Decatur with my daughter and on the way home
I got a phone call from my husband. It seemed that he'd *lost*
Dad. He said that Dad (as usual) wanted to "Go back home,"
and left the house. He followed but Dad was walking so slowly
that Jimmy went around the block and when he came back
Dad was gone. When I got home Jimmy and I went around
the neighborhood, house to house, looking for him while Gina
stayed at home waiting for phone calls. Finally, someone called
to tell us they had him. He'd gone across 127th street and was
covered with mud because he'd fallen in a ditch.

Dad was happy to see us, but was clearly afraid of Jimmy.
Jimmy was mad at himself for losing Dad and mad at Dad
because he'd wandered off. He was frightened that something
might have happened today. Jimmy was very short with Dad
when we finally found him.

February 4, 2003

Gina called me at work this morning to tell me that Grandpa has been up since 5 a.m. He's mad at her because she won't "call the bus company." I kept her on the phone till I got home. When I got there I gave Dad his coffee but he was still mad—now, because *I* wasn't calling the bus company.

He ranted on saying, "The bus just left and there are no more drivers! A woman is waiting for the bus!" I told him I had no idea what he was talking about, but he was mad and wouldn't listen to me. He got louder and angrier. Periodically, he'd say "Fine!" and then refuse to talk to me for a while. Then he'd start all over again.

I finally got him settled in his chair and gave him his coffee. Then he accused me of trying to get him *fired*. As I poured the coffee, he threw the it at me and spilled it all over the table. I poured another cup, hoping to calm him but he continued to complain and argue. Sometimes I argued back and sometimes I ignored him. I made him sit in his chair and would not let him get up. He ranted and raved about the army and how he fought two world wars for scum like me.

He can really talk a person down when he gets like this. He said he was going to call the police and grabbed the TV remote controller to use as something to talk into. He pretended to take some imaginary "thing" from his belt. He would "talk" into that and then put it back. He yelled and whistled for the police.

Dad was really frightening me, so I called Jimmy and gave the phone to Dad. He told Jimmy to get home quickly; that he was on the floor bleeding. But when Jimmy tried to talk to him he told Jimmy to "shut up" and refused to talk any more.

I had to take Gina to school and Dad *would not* get up out of his chair. I was tired and didn't want to fight with him any more, so I left him at home. When I got back I found Dad in the laundry room pulling clean clothes out of the basket and mixing them with the dirty ones. Then Jimmy came home and started yelling at him. It surprises me that Dad is afraid of Jimmy and actually *listens* to him.

I feel bad because I should never have called Jimmy. It's just too hard on him to see his father like this. I was afraid that Jimmy would get into a car accident on the way home.

Dad finally did calm down and I went to the Daycare center with no problems.

February 5, 2003

These last two days have been terrible. Jimmy has actually had to take off work. Dad's been really delusional—seeing things, talking to the TV remote (using it like a walkie-talkie), calling the bus company to pick up people, yelling for the police, and running away. He's been telling the neighbors that we're trying to throw him out of his house, that we want his house and money. He also told the neighbors that I have men over and party and swear all the time, and that I don't cook him anything to eat. He claims that I don't take care of him, that he does the cooking, laundry, and dishes. He says he *does not need us here* and he wishes we would leave.

This morning he sat in the driveway, while it was zero degrees outside, yelling (to anyone who might listen) that he'll die this way and he won't come into the house because he wants the neighbors to see him die and it will be all my fault.

I called the doctor today and asked to increase his dosage of Risperdal. We hope he'll be better in a couple of weeks. Our work is certainly cut out for us. These past few days have been harder for us because he was so good last week. I'm trying to figure out what (if anything) brought this on. I was gone last Saturday and came home on Sunday night. I'm wondering if that put him off his schedule.

All I can do is take one day at a time and make the most of it. If it is a bad day, then I must look for the one good thing and just think of that.

February 6, 2003

Last night Dad had trouble sleeping and urinated on himself three times. Each time I had to get up and change his clothes. Finally, I put on my robe and laid down in his bed so that we would both get some sleep. I did get him to take a bath this morning.

Today I decided to be more creative. I use glass dinnerware and cups here, but I have a few plastic pieces left over from when my children were little. After I gave him his coffee, I filled the sink with clean plastic glasses and bowls and soapy water. He got up after his coffee and did the dishes. Then I put towels in a basket for him to fold and, while he did that, I was able to clean the bathrooms and vacuum the bedrooms without him getting into something.

I dropped him off at Daycare. Later, when he came home, he simply could not sit still and eat. So I put more dishes in the sink and he washed dishes again. While Dad was busy, Jimmy finished putting the final locks on doors to keep Dad from getting hurt or playing with something he shouldn't.

I ran to the store and found a child's kit to make a birdhouse. I sat there with Dad and we put it together. He complained, but he finally got it together. Then I made him paint it. I've discovered that someone really has to monitor Dad and be with him almost all the time now. But it beats having him wandering around the house.

Remember that life is a learning lesson. Take the gift from God and learn from it and be there for someone. If life happens to deliver a situation that you cannot handle, do not attempt to resolve it. Kindly put it in the SFGTD (Something For God To Do) box. All situations will be resolved, but in God's time, not ours. Once the matter is placed in the box, do not hold onto it by *worrying*. Instead, focus on all the other wonderful things that are present in your life now.

February 12, 2003

Today Joe and I went to Joliet, Illinois to see his sisters-in-law. We all went to lunch and then went to the nursing home to see the other sister. When we got home, I took him to the

Daycare Center, around 1:15, so I could have a little break. When I went back to pick him up I found the door locked again. The aides said that while the others were leaving Dad kept trying to escape. They also told me he was very agitated today. As I was trying to get him into the car he decided to fight with me. He had me by my hair and I couldn't get free. Finally someone from the Center noticed us in front and four other women had to help me get him into the car. Then, every time I locked the front door, he unlocked it and opened it. Finally, the five of us managed to get him in the back seat where I have child safety locks on the doors and he can't unlock them. I tried to explain to him that I was taking him home but he refused to listen. He argued all the way home so I turned the radio up to drown him out.

By the time I got him home he had calmed down considerably. The Daycare Center called to make sure he was all right. They were afraid that we wouldn't make it home safely and suggested that I call a neurologist to prescribe some different medication.

My feeling is that he had too much stimulation today. I got him totally off his regular schedule and tried to do too much too short a time. I am still learning.

February 13, 2003

Well today I decided to leave him alone. I drew his bath and made him change his clothes. Later I gave him his coffee but after that I left him alone. I took him to the Daycare Center at noon. When I came to pick him up at 4 p.m. he was sitting on the ground with three men over him in the Daycare driveway. He had managed to escape and was trying to cross Cicero Ave., a pretty busy street. I managed to get him into the van and told him how disappointed I was in him. The Daycare people said I only get one more chance for him to stay there. Also, they want me to change his hours to earlier in the day. They think maybe the sound of the vans starting up is frightening him and making him worry that no one is coming to get him.

It is so hard to work around him and I'm often not sure I am doing a very good job. Dad gets so terrible at times that it's hard to deal with him, both physically and mentally.

I try to remember that, through it all, we have to thank God for each day. I can't wait till I get to talk to God and ask him some questions about things here on earth that I don't understand. Remember to pray and God will lift all from your shoulders and help you with compassion.

February 14, 2003

Do you ever question yourself about decisions you've made or how you've talked to or treated someone? When I get angry with Dad and don't want to talk to him, later I think that maybe I was being unfair. I begin to think that maybe I *don't see* what I think I am seeing or that maybe *I'm* going crazy. But today at Daycare I talked with the owner and she confirmed that all the things that I warned her about Dad are true. Yes, he sneaks and lies and argues constantly. She agrees that it is good to walk away and not talk to him when he's like that.

She said she hasn't seen many people with Alzheimer's who are as bad-tempered as he is. He talked her husband into opening the door a bit because "he couldn't breath and needed some air." And as soon as door was cracked, Dad took off. She also can't believe how strong he is. He argues, sometimes, with the aides just as he does with us at home. They have learned to ignore him when he is in those moods. She agreed that I must really have my hands full.

It was a relief to hear someone else confirm what I know to be true. It's hard because Dad can put on such a good front, sometimes, for other people. Well this is just a note to say how much better I feel since someone else sees these events and behaviors.

February 19, 2003

This week Dad has been calmer. He does not concentrate like he used to. Now, when I give him puzzles to do, he sort of fights me because he doesn't know how to do them. If I am firm with him, however, he'll begin and finally manage to concentrate and finish them. I have him complete three puzzles: one with shapes; one with numbers; and one with the alphabet. He tends to complain like a child and I have to sit with him or he'll quit. But this beats having him wondering around the house.

He's been real antsy lately, wandering around and getting mad when I follow him. I can't seem to get him to fold towels any more. He'll fold a couple and then complain that there's "no hurry to have them done" and that he'll do them tomorrow. He'll say, "I don't have to." Then he just walks away. If I ask him to vacuum, he tells me that he doesn't do a good enough job. But he does still like to clean the kitchen sink—over and over again.

Today, at Daycare, they said that Dad was very good. I found him sitting with his coat on, waiting for me. It's hard for them to keep him focused. He's really not a "people person" and he doesn't seem to like people. He says "Hi" and smiles, but after a bit he just sits quietly and goes off into some "other" land, drifting away from conversations.

Now, when I drop him off, they all say 'Security Alert' and start locking all the doors. At home we have the garage door and the laundry door locked so he won't get hurt. He likes playing in his room. He walks up and down the hall, rearranges his drawers or his closet and takes toilet paper and wipes off his dresser.

He constantly invites Jimmy and me to spend the night after we pick him up from Daycare. And he still asks, all the time. "How are my kids?" and "Why don't they call?" He's pretty confused much of the time now, with an extremely short attention span.

I also discovered that we can't leave items like a 2-liter bottle of pop out, because he'll open it and drink right out of the bottle.

He takes his electric razor apart and then hides it. So now we have to hide his razor and make sure we take it right back when he's not using it.

Through all of this I am learning about my shortcomings and becoming a better person. Jimmy and I are becoming closer, depending on each other more than ever before. God is good. Hopefully we are receptive to his lessons and learning what we are suppose to. Live each day like it is the last. Show compassion. Tell someone you love him or her.

February 25, 2003

Now Dad is on 1 mg of Risperdal a day. I see a big difference in his behavior. I'm not sure if this is a result of the medicine or the disease. He seems to have no sense of direction any more and, having been a truck driver, that's seems pretty significant. He still remembers that the sun rises in the east but when we're in the car he is more confused than ever. He reads the street signs, now, like a child does. When I tell him something, I often have to repeat it a couple of times.

He does like to eat and seems to always have an appetite. Half an hour after a meal, however, he'll be back at the refrigerator looking for food—because he doesn't remember eating.

He doesn't seem to remember where his bedroom is and when I take him to it, he's happy and relieved to know that he has someplace to sleep. Speaking of which, he seems to be sleeping better at night now. When he wakes up to use the bathroom and I tell him to go back to bed, he doesn't fight me any more. He also doesn't seem to know where the toilet is until I show him. He found his razor in the bathroom and decided to shave his forehead and eyebrows.

He doesn't talk much about dancing any more and he doesn't dance in the car as he used to when I play my air drums. He also doesn't recognize stores and buildings that he's seen all his life.

When I draw his bath he still has pride and doesn't want me around while he bathes. I just put in his new clothes and take our the dirty ones so he won't be confused when he gets dressed. He can still dress, feed and bathe himself. He loves to spend lots of hours in front of the mirror combing his "hair" (he wears a wig). He doesn't spend as much time shaving as he use to. In fact, he doesn't seem interested in shaving much at all.

Anyway this is the finding on the disease as it is progressing. It breaks my heart to see him so helpless. But I am so happy that I am here to take care of him.

March 7, 2003

As Dad's disease progresses he becomes more and more confused. He doesn't remember that he ate a meal. When I tell him it is time for bed, he asks me, "What did I do wrong?" and "Why won't you feed me" Then he goes on, "That he's a man who fought *two* wars and do I know how old he is?" If I ask him, of course, he can't tell me.

The medicine is beginning to lose its effectiveness and he's starting to get up at night. The Daycare aides tell me he's getting agitated again, arguing a lot. It took a couple of them to settle him down. My daughter found Dad putting toothpaste on his face and using her eyebrow trimmer to cut his beard.

He forgets why he went into the bathroom. Sometimes he'll go in and then walk right back out. When I ask him what him what he's doing, he'll say, "I have to go to the bathroom." I will take him in and show him the toilet, but he doesn't seem to hear me or understand. So I'll take down his pants and sit him on the toilet. This usually angers him and he'll say, loudly, "Lady, what are you *doing*. I am a *man*. Do you have any idea how *old* I am. Christ's Sakes, let me die *now*. Look at what she is doing to me."

This morning I found him in the bathtub, washing himself with creme rinse instead of soap. He wouldn't listen to me when I explained that he wasn't using *soap*. So I washed his private parts with the soap while he protested. Then I left and let him play in the bathtub while he continued to argue and complain long after I left the room.

It is amazing how he can be so angry when I'm changing or cleaning him, but once I put food in front of him. he tells me, "You are the sweetest thing in the world." I still keep the plastic dishes in the sink and he seems to love to play with them. He washes the counter tops over and over again.

We still play with the puzzles and the cards and, of course, at first he fights because he doesn't want to pay attention and work to put them together. He usually listens to me and then gets into it and does them all. It takes time and I have learned to *slow down* at night. I do bills or crochet while he is working his puzzles.

He's having serious trouble with conversations. He repeats the same thing over and over again. Sometimes what he says simply doesn't make any sense. You can see that he's trying very hard to say something but it just doesn't come out right.

He also gets into the refrigerator if you don't watch him. As I was typing this I suddenly noticed that he was no longer in his chair. I walked into the kitchen and found him drinking the milk right out of the carton. He seems to have an accident almost every night. He can't seem to make it to the bathroom and wets himself and the carpeting.

You can see he's *restless* and doesn't know *what* to do or even what he *can* do. He's combing his wig so much it's starting to get bald. I don't worry about this because it keeps him busy. He loves to spend a lot of time in front of the mirror.

One day this week, I got very excited because when Jimmy drove up, Dad said, "Hey! Look! There's Jimmy! Hey, man, how are you?" Yet when either Jimmy or I pick him up from Daycare, he never seems to know who we are. He'll ask us if we'll take him home and if we want we can stay and have a drink or even spend the night.

I think he recognizes my face as the person who takes care of him, but has no idea, at all, that I'm his daughter-in-law. Whenever I have to take him to a doctor or health professional, he puts on an act like he knows what's going on. So I'll ask him, for their benefit, "Who am I?" Although, he can't tell them, he's still a charmer!

If you don't know him, he can fool you for a little while with the witty things he says. People will ask him, "Hey Joe, how are you?" And he'll reply, "If I was any better, there would be two of me!" It's amazing that he can remember something like that when he's so confused about most daily events.

When I clean house I find empty pop or milk bottles hidden in the closets. Sometimes I find food hidden under his pillow.

It is so cold out now that when he wants to go outside, he usually comes right back in. This is just an update on how the disease is progressing.

March 8, 2003

This was a tense Saturday morning. I finally fell asleep after working through the night, 14 hours. I'd been asleep for less than an hour when Jimmy awakened me because he couldn't find Dad's razor. I told him I hid it under the cushion of the small couch. He looked and came back to tell me that he still couldn't find it. He says that I must have put it somewhere else, so I responded with, "Well, you let Dad wander around last night. Maybe he found it and hid it again."

Finally, I had to get up and look. I found it in Dad's closet behind his some clothes. He must have discovered it and then hidden it himself. Jimmy is very angry now.

It's hard on a family when they must care for a person with Alzheimer's.

March 15, 2003

Well, it snowed again and I had to shovel the driveway yesterday. It's really cold outside but it looks pretty when the sun shines on the snow and it sparkles. Dad wanted to go outside with me, so I put on his coat, hat and gloves and took out a folding chair for him to sit on. He was so funny, trying to tell me where to shovel. Then, he'd say it was too cold and would go back inside, but a few minutes later he'd walk back out again. He did this the entire time I shoveled the driveway.

Regina celebrated her 16th birthday today. First, her girlfriend, Lindsey, from Oklahoma City, flew in for the weekend. They had fun playing in the snow. Later that night Gina, Lindsey and Jimmy went to a Bulls game. He'd gotten them matching t-shirts and caps with the Bulls' logo. I stayed home with Dad.

We did take Dad out to eat at Giordano's restaurant for some great Italian pizza. He watched as we sang *Happy Birthday* to Gina, and smiled when he got a piece of cake. Dad still loves his sweets.

March 23, 2003

Took Dad to a Neurologist and—surprisingly enough—he said he *thinks* that Dad might have Alzheimer's. (Don't they *listen* to us?) He decided to put him on a medication called Donepezil.

Jimmy and I discussed changing Dad's medication. Jimmy isn't sure about this because Dad is easier to get along with now. I have him on a regular routine and I'm even getting more sleep than when we first moved here. He's used to me putting him to bed. I make him use the bathroom first so he'll sleep a little longer before he has to get up again. When he does get up, I can whisper to him that everyone is still sleeping and he usually co-operates and goes back to bed. He's not fighting me now when I give him a bath in the morning and, since we're getting closer, he doesn't seem uncomfortable when I help him undress or bathe.

I'm able to keep him from wandering so much with the puzzles and cards.

I decided to try the medicine, after all, to see if it helped Dad. So far it doesn't look good. Dad's not sleeping at night and he's hallucinating again. Last night, he slept for three hours and then spent the rest of the night talking and raving about "a crane" and "that he didn't know how to do this job," and "we need to understand that this job is new to him."

I think I'll take him off the new medication and see what happens. Maybe this is a side affect of the new prescription or, possibly, the two medications working together.

Be an angel, practice random acts of kindness.

April 13, 2003

I think the secret is to keep him busy. If he's busy, then he can't wander around aimlessly. His mind is focused. When he is not busy he hallucinates and walks in circles not knowing who or where he is.

The morning is pretty easy now. I actually have him on a set schedule. Get up, get him to the bathroom, take a bath (even though he complains); "Cripes sakes! I'm not doing this anymore. Too much work." I dress him in an undershirt and put shaving cream on his face. Then I let him shave, brush his teeth, and get dressed. All of this takes at least two hours. This keeps him busy and focused.

Then we have breakfast and he is like a kid with a treat. After breakfast he goes to Daycare and the morning is basically gone.

The hard part comes in the evening. I don't actually have a regular routine yet. Sometimes he'll watch T.V. Sometimes he just wants to wander. Sometimes he's confused and mean. Sometimes he'll do his puzzles and cards if I sit with him while he works. I know the secret is a routine, I'm having trouble finding and maintaining one as the day moves on.

I've found that it's important to take Dad to Daycare because, even though he may put on his coat and wait for us long before we're supposed to return, I think it's good for him to leave the house for a few hours. He seems more confused on Saturdays, when we're home all day. For some reason, leaving the house and then "coming back home," seems to help

*Dad and Aunt Ann (Joe's sister-in-law) at the Park,
Illinois, April 2003.*

him focus on where he is. When he's home all day he'll get confused and ask us, "Can I go home, now?" or tell us, "I need to go back to work now."

On Thursdays, I go in and do their hair for some of the ladies at the Daycare Center. While I'm there I get to see, first hand, what Dad does in the morning. Believe it or not, there are some men who are actually happy to see him! The staff calls him 'Smokey Joe.' Sadly, Dad doesn't know who they are. He smiles when they call his name and has short conversations with them. But after about an hour and a half, he begins to look for his coat and wants to go home. As I work and mingle with the crowd, Dad says "Hi" to me. He acts like he hasn't seen me in ages and then tells people that he knows me.

He doesn't seem interested in playing games or exercising or painting. Sometimes he'll listen to an aide read the newspaper and sometimes he'll just fall asleep.

Now that the weather is getting warmer and sunnier, he wants to be outside. He likes to walk down the driveway to the mailbox and back to the house, back and forth, back and forth.

I made him walk around the block the other day. I carried his walker because I knew he would be tired. I was right; he walked about a block and then asked for it.

He seems to eat a lot but not at one time. He eats lots of small meals. I will make a big meal and he will eat a little of it, cover it with a napkin. and half an hour later come back and finish it. He can have a glass of pop on the table and get up for something. He'll forget he has a drink and make another one. I've seen him pour cold coffee in his glass of pop and drink it. Of course, I stop him. He gets mad when I do this but it must taste terrible.

He seems to be doing a little better at night. I'm making him go to the bathroom and urinate before I put his pajamas on and tuck him in bed. And it varies, somewhat, how often he gets up in them middle of the night.

Joe at the park, on a beautiful spring day.
Palos Heights, Illinois, April 2003.

April 29, 2003

As the disease progresses, I've noticed that Dad is a lot calmer and a slower. His mind does not always connect now and he's not sure what he's doing. For example, he'll tell me that he's going outside but then he gets sidetracked, forgets and wanders into his bedroom where he ends up going through his drawers. Sometimes he doesn't know what a towel or a toilet is.

I try to make him do as much for himself as possible. He doesn't always like that and usually would rather I do it for him. When I put shaving cream on his face, for instance, he'll stand there with his eyes closed, waiting for me to shave him. I'll tell him that he has to shave himself. He can do this little chore but prefers not to.

Later, in the middle of the day, he'll be upset because he can't find his electric razor. He's hidden it and can't remember where it is, of course. He also can't remember that he already shaved this morning.

I've noticed that his appetite has grown. When I feed him dinner, at five, he'll ask again, at seven, "What do I have for his dinner?" If I tell him he already ate, he'll pout like a child until I give him something to eat. I also have to give him a snack before bed.

I'm noticing that if he starts to wander a lot in the evening before bed, it's harder to get him to stay in bed later that night. His mind is telling him he is *supposed* to be somewhere. But if I keep him busy and his mind occupied, then it's easier to get him to bed. He also seems to sleep better if I tuck him than if he goes to bed on his own.

He is very forgetful, now, with little things. He can have a cup of coffee by his chair and will get up and pour himself another cup. He'll pour pop in his coffee cup, while coffee is already in there. He'll walk back and forth between the bathroom and the living room but he'll forget why he headed for the bathroom in the first place.

He's gotten shorter and walks very slow now. Sometimes I have to remind him to use his knees when he walks. Although, when he looks at me, I can tell that he has no idea who I am, he senses that he's being taken care of.

Sometimes I make him go for a ride with me because I don't want to leave him alone. He gets upset at that and tells me he can take care of himself and doesn't need anybody. But often, he loves to go for short car rides.

As his mind continues to deteriorate, he becomes less and less the person we grew up with. We now call him Joe instead of Dad. If I call him Dad. he doesn't seem to respond. Yet, if Gina calls for her Dad, then Joe will answer and she'll have to tell him that he's her Grandpa.

It's hard to have a conversation with him because he often makes no sense when he talks. When he says something, we usually have no idea what he is saying, but we try to figure it out. He generally tells me, now, when he's going outside or to the bathroom, much like a child. He has no idea how to turn lights on and off or where to find tissue to wipe his nose.

He's just like a grown child who once was very intelligent.

I don't want anyone to feel sorry for me because I choose to do this. I enjoy watching him and taking care of him. It was hard at first, but I got the hang of it, just as we all do with the things that life brings.

Remember that: to the world you are but one person, but to one person you may be the world. Life is short. Take it by the horns and do what you can for other people and enjoy what you can. There is so much beauty out there, but everyone is too busy to see and enjoy it. So take each day and live it like it is your last. Show love and compassion, and most of all, be an angel and show random acts of kindness.

May 1, 2003

Thursday, May first, and it is now time to put adult diapers on Dad at bedtime. He can't seem to leave the bed before he wets himself and the carpet, and this happens at least three times a night.

This morning, as I ran the bath water in the tub, he asked me three times, "What do you want me to do?" I told him I wanted him to take a bath. Each time, he replied, "Well, you'll have to tell me how to do it because I've never done this before."

When I finally got him in the bathtub, he really seemed clueless. When he asked me what he was supposed to do with the washcloth, I tried to make him think. Finally he said that he should put soap on the washcloth, but he claims to have never washed before. When I showed him what to do, he became upset and swore at me. Finally, I left him alone but continued to check on him. While he was washing, he complained, saying, "I don't *know* what you want me to do."

We are all noticing that the disease seems to be progressing much more rapidly now. Jimmy told me that Dad asked him where the bathroom was. I know this is hard on Jim to see his Dad like this. It's frightening how much he's changed since we moved here in August. I didn't expect it to progress so fast.

May 13, 2003

I have found out that people with this disease do not like change. Since we moved here, we've had to go through a lot of changes in the way we live. We've all learned to change in order to live around Dad. He likes it quiet so we've learned to be a lot quieter and more subdued than usual.

However, on Sunday night our daughter, Jessica, came home from college. Dad is having a hard time accepting this change. Because there are no more bedrooms, we closed the sliding door, which separates the family room from the dining room, and Jessica has put her bed and dresser there. There's a lot of giggling and talking and singing going and a lot more excitement in the air. Dad doesn't seem to like this.

I was at work, recently, and when I finally found time to check my phone, I had several calls from my kids. Evidently, Dad had told them that they had to leave and could not live there anymore. They said he wasn't making much sense—that sometimes he thought he was in his house and sometimes he thought he was at work.

This is going to be hard on Joe, but I also have five children and am here for them as well.

I finally got home at 11:00 p.m. and Dad seemed very happy to see me. I made him go to the bathroom and get ready for bed. I thought maybe that was all he needed—his habit at night. But Gina said that Dad was up at 5:00 a.m. and came into her room. She had to chase him out. Then he decided to go through the house, turning on all the lights. She followed him and turned them back off.

He was not happy with me this morning as we went through our routine of bathing, shaving, dressing and so forth. Daycare still does him good, because he always seems better when he's been away from home for a few hours. We barbequed tonight and he seemed to love that. But later, I went running, and when I came back to the house I found him getting into the cars. I guess we'll have to keep them locked.

Tonight he seems to be in a better mood. Remember that life is short. Take time to smell the roses. Enjoy your loved ones. That is really all that counts.

May 16, 2003

Dad is more confused than ever. He has no idea how to turn on the T.V. set or stove. He no longer knows how to make coffee—something he's done his entire adult life. He forgets where the bathroom is. He asks me what he is supposed to do in the bathtub. He's now having trouble with zippers and hooks on his pants. I must look for some elastic waist pants for him to wear. He still loves to eat and is gaining some weight.

He does get mad at me when I don't let him eat as much as he wants, but I have to watch that he doesn't gain too much weight.

May 18, 2003

Today is Sunday. Here is Dad's current schedule. Dad wakes up around 7:00 a.m. I walk him to the bathroom and put him on the toilet. I take off his clothes and run the bath. He asks me, "Why is the water running?" and "What am I supposed to do?" I help him into the bathtub and when he sits on his bath chair, he asks, "What should I do now?" I tell him to wash up and he asks me how. I give him a wash cloth and soap. He says, "How do I do this? Where do I start?" He really doesn't seem to know.

When we're through with the bath, I help him out of the tub. I have his underwear and a towel waiting for him. He dries off himself but, if I don't supervise this, he'll be playing with the water in the bathtub with his towel. After he gets his underwear on, I put shaving cream on his face and give him a razor. I leave him alone and he shaves. When he's done, I put toothpaste on his toothbrush and he brushes his teeth.

Then I lead him back to the bedroom where I have his clothes laid out and tell him to get dressed. Finally, after he's dressed, I tell him to come to the kitchen where I have his coffee waiting for him. I give him his medicine and make him a big breakfast, usually waffles, hash browns, and sausage. He just loves to eat breakfast. After he's eaten, he'll walk around and wash his plate, cup and fork. (I always put these in the dishwasher, later, because they're not really clean.)

At 11:00 a.m., I take him to the Daycare Center. He still seems to benefit from that. He always asks, "Where we are going?" Sometimes I tell him we're going to run errands or get a bite to eat. Once I told him we were going to see his friend. He replied, "I don't have any friends," and added. "I don't want to go."

At 3:00 p.m., we pick him up and when we get home he always has to have a snack. After he eats, he sits in his chair and then goes outside where he walks to the mailbox at the end of the driveway. He walks back and forth and back and forth. By 5:00, we're ready for dinner, which he also loves to eat.

After dinner, he sits in his chair and sometimes wants to fall asleep. We never let him do this, however, because then he won't sleep at night. So he usually gets back up and goes outside and walks around.

He uses the bathroom by himself but can't do the snap and zipper anymore. This really frustrates him. He forgets how to turn the lights on and off and has no idea how to turn the T.V. or radio on and off. We keep the garage door and the laundry door locked all the time. Around 7:00, he'll ask me if I have anything for him to eat. He doesn't remember eating dinner. If I tell him he just ate, he gets an attitude, so I try to give him a fruit snack. Then, sometimes he'll watch T.V. If he starts to "wander" around the house, then I make him do his puzzles and cards.

Finally, at 9:00, I walk him to the bathroom, pull down his pants and sit him on the toilet. Then I lead him to his bedroom, take off his clothes and put on his pajamas and diaper. I put him to bed and tell him to close his eyes to go to sleep. I kiss him on the forehead and remind him to stay in bed till morning.

I turn off the light and close the door. Of course, like a child, he'll get up and wander around his room. I'll put him back in bed. The baby monitor still lets me know when he gets up. This is a typical day now.

May 20, 2003

Dad got up a couple of times last night and when I put him back to bed, even though he's wearing a diaper now, I'll find both him and the bed wet. It's a good thing I have a plastic cover on the mattress. Now he's having trouble with the bathroom during the day. I'm not sure if he forgets or if he's having trouble getting his pants undone. I'm having real trouble finding elastic waist pants with no zipper. I don't want sweat pants or nylon pants. I always see people in nursing homes wearing these, but Dad never wore pants like that.

I still think that maintaining a regular schedule and making him do simple things keeps him from roaming too much, both physically and mentally. Maybe I'm just fooling myself, but I hope a routine will keep him with us a little longer, mentally. I think he deserves whatever I can do to maintain a quality of life.

I'm afraid I'll have to start using the diapers in the daytime as well as at night. He told Jimmy he doesn't want to think for himself and wants people to think for him. That is not the Joe I know.

May 22, 2003

Today is Thursday and it was a hard day. Dad is now more confused than ever. He's rushing but he's unable to concentrate on anything at all. When I put him in the bathtub this morning, he snuck out. I had to put him back in and wash him. He was mad that *he* had to shave and brush his teeth, something we do every morning. He was very disturbed by this. He did not want to put on the elastic waist pants and forgot how to put his shirt on.

He asked me what was on his plate for breakfast. He complained that I wasn't making it fast enough. He wants me to cut up his waffles now—this is another turning point.

June 21, 2003

As the days go by now, our routine doesn't seem to be helping him anymore. He doesn't seem to remember how to do anything or maybe he just doesn't want to remember. He still fights me when I make him take a bath. It's been almost a year now and you'd think that he'd be used to this. When I leave the bathroom, he sneaks out of the bathtub. When I come back to check, he'll be dry and there's no towel in the bathroom. He tells me that he's already washed up and that the water "dissolved into his skin."

After he's had breakfast, he'll ask me, "When can I shave?" Of course, he doesn't remember that we did this already. He's always excited about going for a car ride, but after about ten minutes, he begins to complain and begs me to go home. He still likes to wash dishes. Now he looks for the glass dishes (that we use everyday) and I have to catch him before he puts them away dirty. He has no idea what a dishwasher is, so I'm safe there.

He still forgets when he ate and asks to eat again an hour later. I ran out of Risperdal recently and I was quickly reminded of how much that medicine helps Dad. Without the Risperdal, he wouldn't sleep and became verbally abusive again. I was glad to get him back on the medication.

I'm now putting a restrainer on him at night so I can sleep. He's managed to get out of it, but I'm still experimenting with different ways to tie it. I don't use this every night, just the nights when he refuses to sleep.

He still needs to walk to the mailbox and back, no matter how dark it is outside.

It's hard to do things as a family now, because he complains so much.

Sometimes I can get through it and sometimes it gets to me. Then I get mad at myself for being so selfish. For Father's Day, we went miniature golfing. I was hoping that he could play along with us, but he complained so much that we told him to sit in a chair and watch the greens where he could watch us. But he kept getting up and looking lost, unable to find us. So I made him walk the 18 holes with us and he was upset because he wanted to sit. It does make for a tiring day.

Celebrating Father's Day, with Miniature Golf, June 2003.
Left to Right: Jimmy, Joe, Jessica, Adias, and Regina.

Dad is spending a lot of time outside now that it is warmer and, to my surprise, he's not running away. He's busy raking leaves and branches out from under the bushes. My son Erik is getting married soon and we'll have to put him in a nursing home for a couple of days while we go to the wedding. He's not alert enough to travel and he'll make it the event very difficult for us if we take him. I wish the old Joe was with us so Erik could have grandparents from both sides of the family there.

We cannot take life for granted. You never know what is going to happen tomorrow and how you will be living. So you have to really live today like it is your last.

June 28, 2003

Well this Saturday brought a change of events. Last night I left Gina to watch Dad because Jimmy and Jessica are out of town and I was working. I came by to check up on them and put Dad to bed. He didn't know why, at 10:30 p.m., he had to go to bed. I used the restrainer in order to keep him down. I don't tie this very tight and within minutes he got out and was roaming up and down the hall. Gina called me at work, asking me to come back because she was scared and Grandpa wouldn't go to bed. So my partner and I returned. We tied him in the bed again, while Dad chanted, "Holy Father, Mother Mary! Look at what they are doing. They are trying to kill me."

Of course we tried to explain to him that there were no adults around to watch him and we couldn't have him roaming around the house. We told him that he was supposed to be sleeping now. Of course he didn't understand anything of what we were saying. We had to get back to work so I called Gina, a little while later. She said that he was still chanting and yelling that we were trying to kill him.

I got home at 6:00 a.m. and turned on the baby monitor. He was fidgeting around in his bed. I went to sleep at 7:00 and got up at 8:00. I could hear that he was still restless. When

I went into his bedroom to untie him, I found him naked as a jaybird. His pajamas and diaper were on the floor but the restrainer was still around his waist.

He could not physically stand up and I couldn't understand anything he was saying. I made him get dressed. He really had no idea what I was saying. It took him an hour to figure out how to put his socks on. He kept asking me, "Is it the first or the second?" Of course, I had no idea what he meant. Finally he put on his pants while I kept falling asleep in the bed, waiting for him.

I made him his coffee but he never drank it. Finally, I went back to bed and woke up at 12:30 p.m. He was sleeping in his chair in the living room with his pants half-way down and his shirt off. He never drank the coffee. I made him wake up. I dressed him and gave him breakfast and coffee again.

He seems better now that he ate. I can hear him, right now, trying to wash dishes. It was scary to see such a big change in such a short time.

July 16, 2003

What fun is ahead of us, Kristina and her son Damien came up for Erik's wedding. Dad wasn't sure how to react with a baby in the house. He'd just sit in his chair and watch this child and smile. So Kristina showed Damien to Dad and put him in his lap. Dad stayed very still while holding Damien, smiling. For those few moments Dad seemed like a different

Grandpa with his great-grandson, Damien Michael Morris,
Illinois, July 16, 2003.

person. I tried to explain to him that Kristina was his grandchild and the baby belonged to her, making him his great-
grandchild.

Dad would smile and nod his head but I'm not sure he
understood what I was telling him. Then he looked up and
put his arms forward, trying to let us know that we should
take the baby back.

It does hurt to know that Dad will not get to enjoy his
great-grandson and it really hurts that we can't take him to my
son's wedding.

July 24, 2003

I've seen many changes in Dad lately. First, he doesn't stand
still anymore. He has to rock back and forth on each foot.
When he sits in his chair, he either moves his legs up and down
or rocks himself in the chair. He doesn't seem to want to go
anywhere without asking permission. He still loves to go for
car rides and asks to go along with me anytime I leave. But just
as soon as we get to our destination, he immediately wants to
come home.

For example, I'll say I am going to the park for a walk and
he'll act like an excited child and beg to go. Shortly after we
leave, however, he'll say, "Too far. Take me home." Sometimes
I take him to the park and make him walk anyway but he'll
complain all the way there. When we get to the park, he'll ask,
"What are you going to do with me now?" Then he'll pray
that he can go home.

Four generations: Kristina and Joe with Jimmy holding the new grandbaby, Damien. They arrived for Erik's wedding in July, 2003.

He constantly forgets what he is doing or where he is going. He'll say he's going to the bathroom. Then he'll walk in
his bedroom and come right out again. At bath time, I used to
be able to put him in the bathtub and he would wash himself.
But now he just throws water on his feet, waits for me to leave,
and then drains the water out and gets out of the bathtub.
This means that I must wash him now, while he complains
and prays constantly, telling me to "hurry up" and "that's
enough."

He is very hard-headed. When he's putting on his underwear and I tell him to *sit*, so that he doesn't fall, he won't listen
to me. He has to stand and struggle, almost falling each time
he lifts his leg.

He still walks back and forth to the mailbox or just back
and forth from his chair to the door, which he opens, turns
around and comes right back in again. We can no longer hold
a conversation with him. He doesn't know what we're talking
about and, in any case, he will usually start an argument. One
minute he'll say, "I am staying right here in my chair. I'm not
going out anymore for the night." Then, a minute later, he'll
get up and tell us he's "going outside."

Sometimes, when I make him dinner, if he's in a bad mood,
he can act like a child. He'll say, "This isn't for me." If I try to
tell him that, "Of course it's for you," he'll argue that it is *not*.
When I tell him to slow down and look at me, he'll close his
eyes and pout like a child.

August 19, 2003

Today is Tuesday and I've just learned that we're going to move to sunny Arizona because Jimmy has found a new job there! Dad has been watching us fix up the house, painting and cleaning. He even asks if he can help, although when I give him a job he always decides that, "This doesn't have to be done now." He quits and then says. "I'll do this tomorrow."

We're having people coming in and looking at the house. Dad asks, "What's going on?" Although I tell him that the house is for sale, he just doesn't comprehend what this means.

We try to agree with Dad now and not argue with him. If we do, he gets mad and tells us that "He wants to die right now." Dad is bullheaded and stubborn. This drives Jimmy crazy and sometimes they can really get into it. I think it scares Jimmy that this could happen to his father. Dad still walks to the front door and back to his chair, over and over again, all day. He prays the same prayer at least 200 times a day.

He is having more accidents now, mostly with his bowels. I'm thinking of putting diapers on him more often. We still have our ritual in the morning and at night. At bath time, I wash the top half of his body and he washes the bottom. I want him to do as much as he can before he becomes to dependant.

He's starting to get his clothes mixed up. I caught him yesterday putting his legs into the armholes of his shirt. The he asked me to help pull up his pants. Some days he knows how to put on his socks and some days he doesn't.

September 13, 2003

I finally got angry today. Dad asked me if I would shave his face. He did this, not in so many words, but by putting his fingers on his face and saying, "I have to get rid of it." So I took him in the bathroom, put shaving cream on his face and gave him his razor. He shaved himself but he missed a few spots. So I washed his face and put more shaving cream on his face and told him that he missed a couple of spots. He didn't like that, and said, "No, I'm not going to shave." I told him, "Yes. You're going to finish what you started."

He turned on the water, splashed it on his face and started wiping off the shaving cream. I took him by the hands and told him, "This is what happens to little boys who throw temper tantrums." I put him in his bedroom and locked the door. For 15 minutes he banged on the door and prayed and told me to "Unlock this car door."

Finally, I unlocked the door. I said, "If you throw another temper tantrum again, I'll lock you in the bedroom again." Then back to the bathroom we went. I watched him finish shaving his face.

After this he couldn't keep still. He walked from his chair to the front door where he'd open the door, close it and then walk back to his chair. He kept saying, over and over again, "I need to go outside." Finally I took him outside and down the block. All the while he swore at me, using the f—word. So I brought him back to the house, gave him some water, and he started all over again with this roaming to and from the front door.

September 17, 2003

This is a sad day. It is the last day that I'm going to be able to take Dad to see Aunt Betty, Aunt Yolanda and Aunt Ann. It was just like any normal day as I struggled to get Dad up, fed, bathed, dressed and ready for our lunch appointment with his sisters-in-law. I got Dad in the car and drove to pick up Aunt Ann and Aunt Yolanda. It is always so good to see them. We decided to go see Aunt Betty at the nursing home before we went to lunch. When we got there, they loaned me a wheelchair since walking is getting harder for Dad.

Joe and his sisters-in-law: (l to r) Joe, Yolanda, Anne and (sitting in wheelchair) Betty. We had some fun times together in Illinois and visited often, even after Joe became sick.

I decided it was time to make some memorable pictures for all of them, so I put up my tripod. Dad and Aunt Betty kept looking at each other! Finally, after much coaxing, I got the shot. Then, I thought it would be nice to have a picture with me in it as well. This one turned out to be such a great memory photo! I gave a copy to all three aunts and labeled it "Best Friends."

After we left the nursing home, the four of us went out to eat. I'm going to miss our luncheons, but I'm happy they got to visit regularly for a short time. Remember each day is a GIFT from God to enjoy. Don't put off tomorrow what you can do today!

September 21, 2003

Well, it's been over a year now, as we've watched Dad progress through the advanced stages of Alzheimer's. Last August he could carry on a normal conversation, understand directions, take care of himself, and make coffee. Now he feels the need to ask if he can go outside or to the bathroom. I must bathe him because he doesn't remember how to do this himself. I make him shave and brush his teeth, although I have to keep an eye on him or he'll brush his face instead of his teeth.

I keep adult diapers on him all the time now and he doesn't seem to know the difference. When he has an accident at night and his diaper is too full, he *does* know to take it off but he's confused about putting on a new diaper. Of course bowel movement accidents are difficult for him. He tries to clean the mess but always makes a bigger one.

I have seen this quiet man, who knew so much about life, turn into a bad-tempered child. Even in his own home, he asks where the bathroom is or his bedroom. He seems to be afraid to cross the street without me, which is a blessing.

This is such a terrible disease. It melts the mind. Even though he's relatively healthy, his ability to do even the smallest task is disappearing. It's like watching a special-needs child.

I am sure that the move will produce more confusion for him and, of course, just transporting him that far will be difficult. The nice part, however, is that the weather will always be warm so he can go outside year round. In our new home his bedroom has its own bathroom.

I've found, through my 49 years, that life is challenging and always an adventure. If you pay attention, then there are so many lessons to be learned and ways to help teach others. Using your gifts from God, showing love and compassion to everyone, make for a rewarding life. I have been blessed over and over again. Maintaining an uplifting, positive attitude and staying close to God is the key to a successful and happy life. Yes, sometimes you may fall, but God is always there for you and He will forgive you if you only ask.

September 25, 2003

Today is Thursday, a normal day. Joe wakes up early in the morning with his pajamas and diaper soaking wet. I put dry pajamas on him. Sometimes he goes back to bed and sometimes he just sits in his chair, but he always falls back asleep.

Between 8:00 and 9:00 a.m., I make him coffee and breakfast and give him his Risperdol. I let him sit and drink coffee until about 10:00. Then I coax him into the bathroom, put him on the toilet, take his clothes off and put him in the bathtub (usually under protest). I bathe him and then give him the washcloth and let him rewash himself.

When he gets out of the tub, I make him dry himself. I help him put on his underwear and then I shave his face. I give him his toothbrush and make him brush his teeth. Usually, by this point, he has an attitude. He doesn't like bathing and is often verbally abusive.

I lay his clothes on his bed and make him dress himself. Sometimes he does just fine and sometimes he doesn't know his pants from his shirt. I always make him put on his socks, which he begs me to put on for him. No matter what he says, I know that he can put them on himself.

He always wears a baseball cap. He loves to go for rides and I drive him to the Daycare Center. He still goes there four hours everyday, Monday through Friday. When we bring him home, he comes in the house and sits in his chair. Then he gets up and walks outside, only to return right away to sit in his chair. He repeats this routine over and over again.

His famous saying is. "What do you have for me?" That usually means he wants a pop and food. He is still very forgetful about meals and always wants to eat again an hour after a meal. He just can't remember when he last ate. He can say some mean and nasty things, so I've gotten in the habit of giving him some fruit or applesauce when he asks to eat again.

He likes to drink soda pop all the time, so I try to mix water with the soda to cut down the calories. He doesn't seem to notice this. Now, I cut up his meat during his meals along with anything else that may need cutting. If I don't do this, he'll put the whole thing in his mouth.

Around 8:00 p.m., I give him another dose of Risperdal. He generally goes to bed between 8:30 and 9:00. First I try to coax him into the bathroom. Then I undress him and put on his pajamas (again, this is usually under protest). I make him sit on the side of the bed and slide his legs up into the bed and cover him up.

I turn off the light, give him a kiss on the cheek and close the door, all the while repeating to him that it is time for sleep. Because he no longer remembers how to turn on the lights, being in the dark helps him stay in bed and sleep. Sometimes he even sleeps right through the night.

I don't allow him to walk around during sleep time. I also don't let him take naps during the day. I've found that if he sleeps during the day then he won't sleep at night.

When he uses the toilet now, I make him sit to urinate so he won't mess up his clothes. And I never leave him by himself for more than five minutes.

October 5, 2003

Dear Connie:

I want to send you a copy of Joe's Living Will. Also, I want to tell you a little bit about Joe. He is a 77-year-old male, oriented to his name, but not time or place.

He can still do some of the basic things like going to the bathroom, although I keep adult diapers on him because he has accidents at night and sometimes during the day as well. I make him sit when using the toilet because he will wet his pants otherwise. He doesn't always make it to the toilet when having a bowel movement.

Joe does not know how old he is but sometimes he remembers when his birthday is. He doesn't know my husband (his son) or me (his daughter-in-law) but he recognizes us as the people who take care of him.

When I feed him, I make sure to cut his food up; otherwise he'll try to put the whole piece in his mouth. He cannot stand still. He constantly walks in and out of the house or rocks back and forth when standing or sitting.

I bathe him and shave him but I make him brush his teeth. He always complains, but that is the way he is. He does not like to take baths. He also does not like to have a hairy face. If I miss a day and don't shave him, he's very uncomfortable and lets me know that somehow his face doesn't "feel right."

He also cannot zip up or button his trousers. Occasionally, he can't tell the front from the back of his trousers and sometimes he tries to put his shirt on as if they were pants.

He can talk and sometimes he makes sense; most of the time, now, he does not. He does recite a Catholic prayer all day long. He is a very considerate man. He has good manners and often apologizes. But if you get him mad, he does have a truck driver's mouth.

I put him in his pajamas at night and he does not like that. I make him go to the bathroom so that his diaper and pajamas are not soaking wet in the morning. (Despite this, his pajamas and bed clothes are usually wet.)

You must dress him in the morning and at night or he will wear the same clothes. I make him sleep all night (or at least stay in bed) and don't allow him to wander around until I'm up. I give him his medication (Risperdal) twice a day, one dose with breakfast and one at 8: 00 p.m., shortly before his bedtime.

I have a question for you. Are you going to be in charge of his personal belongings and shaving cream and razor? If you let Joe have them, he'll hide them and you may not find them again.

Although I have not had him formally tested by a doctor, I am sure he is in the second stage of Alzheimer's. I have done a lot of reading on the subject.

He will complain, sometimes, of pain in his right knee. He had a hip operation last December and he probably needs a knee operation. We agreed, however, with the doctor, that surgery would not be in his best interest. He has a hernia in his groin and his testicles are enlarged as a result, but he has no pain or discomfort. He has a sty in his left eye. He's had ointment, eye drops, and medication but nothing seems to get rid of it. The doctor said that he has a lot of infected tear ducts on the upper and lower eyelids. He recommends daily hot compresses and tells me that in time it will heal. I try to do this in the morning when he's taking a bath. Otherwise he is in good health.

I Hope this helps with any questions you may have about my father-in-law.

Sincerely,
Marie Fostino

October 25, 2003

Jimmy flew with Joe to Arizona because it would be too hard to drive that long with Dad in the car. We placed Dad in a nursing home until we got moved into our new house. This is Saturday and we have finally in arrived in sunny Arizona. It is so pretty here. In the morning I can watch the sunrise over the mountains while I work on the computer.

Regina and I traveled on Friday and stayed the night with my good friend, Evett. We visited with my son Erik and his lovely wife Betsy. Then we left early the next morning and arrived at my daughter Kristina's house in Oklahoma on Saturday evening. I got to feed, bathe, and rock to sleep my newest grandbaby. He is so beautiful.

We spent all day on Sunday spoiling Damien and enjoying Kristina. But, early Monday morning, we were back on the road again. We traveled all day on Monday and actually made it to the state of Arizona that evening. We spent the night by the Painted Desert and went to see it on Tuesday morning.

Our real goal was to see the Grand Canyon on the way to our new home. It took four hours but it was worth it. This was such a beautiful sight. The Grand Canyon cannot be described by words, it is so beautiful. We spent some time there and even walked down it a bit.

We arrived at the townhouse, where Jimmy was staying, on Tuesday night and on Friday we finally got to unload the boxes into our new home. We picked Dad up from the nursing home on Sunday and it broke my heart—I could see, right away, that he'd lost weight and was wearing clothes that were not even his (a long-sleeved shirt in 100-degree weather).

But we're slowly getting him back on his old schedule. He has his own room with his own bathroom. He's getting up a lot at night but we're working on getting him to sleep through the night again.

He seems amazed at all the construction going on in the neighborhood and keeps telling me to, "Look at all the *changes*." When we drive down the street and he sees all the palm trees he keeps asking me, "How did *those* get there?"

I tell him that we are in Arizona, but, of course, he doesn't comprehend this.

Anyway, God has been good to us. He looks after us and takes care of us. We are now living in this big beautiful house. Sometimes I feel like I don't deserve it. We have moved so many times and have had so many different kinds and styles of homes. Looking back through the years, it now seems that the homes we had seemed to fit our needs. And this one does also. It is so exciting to be living here and to see new sights again. You just have to love life and believe in God when you see these beautiful sunrises and mountains.

November 6, 2003

I'd like to describe how the disease is progressing. Joe doesn't have any idea that we've moved. We've maintained our morning routine of taking a bath, getting dressed and so forth. When I give him a meal, he still eats it right up. In fact, he inhales it.

When I take him outside for a ride, he loves to look at the mountains. He smiles and tells me, "Just look at that!" he says, "we are in the country."

He still asks about the palm trees he sees everywhere. I'll tell him they are palm trees. I'll say, "Joe, we don't live in Chicago any more. We moved far away and live in Arizona now." But he really doesn't understand what I'm saying.

I've also noticed that he's sleeping more. He seems to stare off into "nowhere," more often. I have to tell him repeatedly to do something before he'll do it.

He'll also ask if he can do something and we have to answer him several times before he understands.

Until recently he could still sign his name. He was a little shaky, but he could do it without a lot of coaxing. Now he's unable to do this without a great deal of help. He must be told what the letters are and, even then, he can't always remember how to make the them.

I finally got a "Handicapped" sign for my car so that when I have Dad with me in the car I can park close to entrances. He does have more trouble walking now. He walks very slowly and many times I must hold his hand and usher him where we're going. I'm learning to really hate it when people abuse their privileges and use those Handicapped Parking spaces. Recently, while I waited for a parking spot to open up, I watched two women and three children, parked in a Handicapped Space, load up their groceries and drive away. There was nothing disabled about any of them. I figure that someone in the family is handicapped and they just use the sign whenever it's convenient.

Then a man drove into a Handicapped Space and hopped out of his car. I just stared at him as I was getting Dad out of the car. He saw me and then just looked at the ground when he passed us. What is wrong with this world? You know, I've heard that you need to be careful for what you wish for—it could just happen to *you*. Why would someone take a parking spot away from a person who has trouble walking? Is this just because he's lazy?

Anyway, Dad seems more "distant" now. He doesn't really talk much, except when he has to use the bathroom or is hungry. I do notice that his diapers are wetter now. He doesn't remember to go to the bathroom regularly, like he used to.

I found him a new doctor and the nurse practitioner says I should try to get him off the Risperdal. I'll try to wean him off it soon, maybe right after Thanksgiving.

I went to the Social Security office and asked that they assign me to be the payee for his checks. I don't understand it but they said they'll want to "check" on him periodically. They also want me to document how I'm spending the money to show that I'm spending it on him. What I don't understand is that when I have him at a nursing home for a couple of days and it costs me $150 a day, nobody asks the nursing home for documentation of this sort. Who cares how I spend the money, so long as Dad is being taken care of? I don't get paid $150 a day to watch him and I know that I take much better care of him than anybody in a nursing home.

Oh well, I guess it is just the normal government red tape. Of course I use his money for him, but I also use it to help with other expenses, since I do watch him and I can't have a regular job to help supplement our income. I'm not complaining—I just don't understand their rules.

Well, this is a new phase we're seeing with Alzheimer's. I do love to watch him these days. He smiles more now. I notice that he watches me all the time. If we're in the family room watching TV or I'm cooking in the kitchen, he's always there, just watching me. He makes me think of a young child whose constantly making sure that his Mom is "still there."

My kids are coming for Thanksgiving and we've planned a trip to the Grand Canyon. I hate to do it, but we'll have to send him to the nursing home while we're gone. I want to have some time to sightsee and explore with the family and if we take Joe with us, then this won't be possible. But they'll be here at the house for a while and will get to spend some time with him.

Remember that life is a gift. Enjoy today and make it count. There is no guarantee what tomorrow may bring. And remember that to the world, you are a small person, but to one person, you may *be* their world.

November 9, 2003

Today Jimmy and I went out for a couple of hours and Jennifer, our 24-year-old daughter, watched Grandpa for us. While she was watching TV, Joe escaped. He just walked out the front door and straight to our neighbor's house where he opened the door walked right inside.

When she got him home, later, he had to go to the bathroom. Evidently he had a bowel movement and Jennifer found him playing in the toilet. I'm sure he thought he was "cleaning" it, but when Jennifer saw the mess and the smell, it made her sick and a little afraid. She locked Joe in his room.

When I got home I cleaned him up and then I cleaned the up bathroom. The next day I found feces stuck on his chair and in the bedroom where he'd hidden them under the pillows.

November 15, 2003

It is beautiful out here in sunny Arizona. If we were in Chicago right now, it would be cold and maybe even snowing. But here it is only sweatshirt weather. Dad is adjusting nicely to his new home. He seems to like taking car rides. I love to point out the cotton fields to him as we drive to our

favorite place to shop. He notices the palm trees and mountains and keeps asking me how they got there. I try to explain
that we've moved to Phoenix, but he doesn't understand.

It's getting harder for Joe to walk long distances now. I
hold his hand and lead him to and from the car. He shuffles
slowly and likes to hang onto something. In the grocery store,
I always give him a shopping cart, which he loves to push. He
seems to enjoy grocery shopping so I try to take him twice a
week. He likes going up and down the aisles but he keeps a
very close eye on me and never lets me out of his sight. It's
difficult to move at his pace so sometimes I run ahead and
gather all the items we need before Joe gets to the end of the
aisle.

We also try to go out to eat at least once a week. We go to
the same place every Wednesday where the staff is getting to
know us. They are very good with Joe. It seems that they always give us the same table and try to fill our orders as quickly
as possible. He's always a bit irritated when he sits down and
sees silverware but no food. They remember to give us crackers and our drinks so he can keep busy until the food arrives.

*Remember this: To the world you are only one person but to
one person you may be the world.*

November 28, 2003

Hope everyone is counting blessings! We all know that there's good and bad in the world and you have to count on seeing some of both. We should try to remember the good, though, and forget about the bad.

Our Thanksgiving was very lively. There were good and bad times but, all things considered, it was great. First, I had to put Dad in a nursing home for three days while we took our trip to the Grand Canyon. So the first bad thing was that Dad couldn't spend that time with us. This made me think about all the holidays we used to spend with him and all the good times we had over the years. I remembered how we'd all go camping and how much fun he was before this terrible disease got the best of him.

The good thing, of course, was that all my kids were here. We had ages ranging from 6 months to 50 years. We all had such a wonderful time together. It was too cold and most of us got sick but that didn't take away from the beauty of the Grand Canyon. Another bad thing was that Jennifer is in the armed services and is going to Turkey and then Iran and will be gone for 12 to 18 months. But the good thing was that this was a fun way to spend time together as a family before she leaves. The date keeps changing but they say now that she'll leave by the 4th of December.

Another good thing was that our daughter, Jessica, got engaged while we were at the Grand Canyon. You should see the rock on her finger! We're happy for them both and Zack is such a nice fellow. We have been so blessed.

I know that we have some difficult times ahead of us, between Dad and Jennifer, but God is taking care of us and I give him all my stress to worry about. I'm starting a new job and, after my training, I'll be working two nights a week, from 9 p.m. to 9 a.m.

Oh yes, and Jennifer is getting baptized this Sunday.

My house has been so full of people for days now. It's been loud and messy and, boy. am I going to miss this when the kids leave! These are the signs of life you know.

December 19, 2003

MERRY CHRISTMAS!

Well, another year has come and gone. In this past year we've certainly had our ups and downs. The other day I remembered something my father-in-law told me, years ago, that I would never forget. He said, "Always rely on *change*. Nothing ever stays the same."

In this year of 2003, Jimmy turned 50-years-old. My daughter, Kristina, and her husband, Arin, had a beautiful baby boy. My parents had their 50th wedding anniversary— a great accomplishment in today's world. My son, Erik, was married to beautiful Betsy. We moved to Arizona. We spent Thanksgiving at the Grand Canyon with all our kids. Jessica got engaged to Zack. Jennifer was deployed and is now in Ft. Bliss and will soon leave for Turkey and, later, Iraq. Regina is now a Junior in high school.

Arizona Christmas, 2003. Left to Right: Jimmy, Marie, Regina, Joe, Jennifer (about to leave for Iraq), Adias, and Jessica.

We must remember that each day is a gift from God. We can only live by his teachings. It is up to us to choose to be happy or not. We are thankful each and every day. Life is an adventure, with ups and downs. Each day, find something good about that day and focus on it. Each day find a bad thing about that day and then give it to God.

December 27, 2003

Christmas is fun this year as we are trying to make it special in our new house in this new state. First, it is warm here. We lived in Oklahoma where the weather is always unpredictable—one day it's warm but the next can be cold. I remember putting up outdoor Christmas lights while bundled up in hat, coat and gloves one year and just a sweatshirt the next. Here in sunny Arizona, it is warm and Jessica and Regina are in charge of decorating the outside of the house. Jimmy is stringing lights on the roof and Adias is putting up our little Christmas town on the center island in the kitchen. Dad is sound asleep through all this.

Next is the chore of making Christmas cookies. I get plenty of help from Adias and, after they're baked, the girls all help Adias decorate them. Our tree is already decorated. Jennifer was told she wouldn't be here, so we celebrated Christmas early, in November. I got a small artificial tree this year and used patriotic decorations. This is the first time I have not had a real tree. I only had three of my children, along with my grandaughter, Adias, home for Christmas.

We are fortunate that Jennifer was able to come back for a few days at Christmas. We had church Christmas Eve and, of course, watched *It's A Wonderful Life.* On Christmas morning we all opened our gifts. Dad just watched what was going on.

Christmas in Arizona, 2003. Dad, Jimmy,
Regina, Jessica, Adias and Jennifer.

Christmas in Arizona, 2003. Joe opens a gift.

He took quite a bit of time opening his presents. He seemed to enjoy putting on his new hats but he *really* liked the jars of cookies we wrapped up. Dad has always loved his cookies. I remember, years ago, when Dad would just have coffee and cookies for breakfast before going to work.

The noise doesn't seem to bother him as he dozes off in his favorite chair.

Christmas dinner is always a delight with turkey and manicotti. This, of course, is still one of Dad's favorite things to do—eat!

January 9, 2004

Every morning now, I see a very confused old man. He is bald and repeatedly says the words, "Mother Mary." When he stands he only comes up to my chin now. He walks in small shuffles. He smells like urine when his pajamas are wet.

I get Joe up every day about 9 a.m. Sometimes I find that he is already up and wandering around in his room. He usually has a great big smile when he sees me. I tell him to come with me to the bathroom. Although he doesn't understand, he follows me and sits on the toilet. I tell him to go to the bathroom and then I start taking off his socks, pajama bottoms and diaper. This usually upsets him and he says, "No! Don't do that. Why are you doing that?"

I take off his pajama top and his undershirt while he's still protesting. I have the bath water running in the tub. He finally urinates in the toilet and I tell him to get into the bathtub. "No, no," he says, "I don't want to go there."

Despite his protests, he does get into the bathtub and I have to tell him, repeatedly, to sit on his bath chair. He looks at it and has to turn his whole body in a complete circle before he sits. Then he asks, "What are we doing here? I don't want this." As I bathe him, he tells me "Alright, that's enough. Let's go, let's go." When I'm finally done I tell him he can get out of the tub. I give him a big towel and ask him to dry himself.

While he is slowly trying to dry himself, I get his clothes and put them on the bed. While I'm moving around his room and making the bed, I hear him say, "Don't go nowhere. Help me." I finish drying him and put some powder on. I help him into his undershirt and make him sit on the chair in the bathroom so that I can put on his diaper.

Then it is time to shave. He really doesn't like me to shave him but he hates having a beard even more. While I put shaving cream on his face, he tells me,"That's enough! Let's go." I shave him but I make him brush his teeth. He is like a child and if I don't watch him, he'll quit or miss his teeth and brush his face. If this happens, then I show him my teeth. This seems to help and he moves the toothbrush back to his teeth again.

When it's time to get dressed, I see he no longer knows the difference between his pants and shirt so I put his shirt on him. I put his socks and pants on the bed and leave his room. He almost always pleads with me, saying. "No! Help me. I can't do it!"

However, he finally comes out with his socks and pants on. I usually have to re-do his socks and then he puts on his shoes. I now have to pull the backs of his shoes up over his heels. Our total bath and dress time takes about an hour.

Of course, the next question is always, "What do you have for me?" He still enjoys his coffee in the morning and he loves to eat.

His behavior varies quite a bit now from day to day. I cannot predict how he is going to be on any given day. Sometimes he's very quiet and will sleep all day in his chair. Some days he wanders all around the house. When he goes outside, I have to watch him closely so that he doesn't go into the neighbor's house.

Some days he's very talkative, although this means that he'll repeat the same phrase over and over again. It might be, "Mother Mary," or something he's seen on the TV, like "Nick." He no longer seems to understand anything I say. He isn't able to really listen, either. He's just in his own little world now. Sometimes he asks where the bathroom is and sometimes he doesn't. When he has a bowel movement, sometimes he'll tell us and I'll change his diaper. Sometimes he'll simply take his pants and diaper off wherever he happens to be and then I'll have a big mess to clean up.

We lock his bedroom door now, at bedtime, since he never sleeps through the night and we need to get some sleep. Sometimes he gets up and yells, "Hello, Hello?" He plays with the doorknob and then, when we don't answer, he quiets down. Sometimes he goes back to sleep and sometimes he just wanders around. I can tell if he was up all night by the way he's rearranged his bedroom and the bathroom.

Sometimes he thinks he is at work, like he used to, but not too often anymore. He still says he needs "to go home," but he's not as upset as he used to be. We just say that we'll take him home tomorrow and that seems to settle him down.

It is amazing how much this fine man has changed with this disease.

A lesson I've learned is not to put off what you can do or say today, because tomorrow may not come. Don't put off any kindness that you can show today.

February 2, 2004

Today was an eventful day for Jimmy. He told me that he was outside for a few minutes doing yard work while he left Dad alone in the house. When Jimmy came back inside he saw Dad standing in the middle of the kitchen, pulling up his pants. Jimmy said he was a little puzzled but thought Dad must have gone to the bathroom and was having trouble pulling up his pants. When he approached to help, he discovered that Dad had just had a bowel movement on the kitchen floor. It seems that he couldn't find the bathroom without Jimmy's help.

February 20, 2004

Jessica was watching Dad today while I was at work and Jimmy was at Culinary School. It seems that when Jimmy came home everything was very quiet except for some muffled yelling. He walked into the family room and asked Regina where Jessica and Grandpa were. Regina just pointed to Dad's room and said, "You'd better get in there."

Jimmy opened the door and the yelling, louder now, was clearly coming from the adjacent bathroom. He opened the bathroom door and got the shock of his life. There was diarrhea all over the bathroom floor and a large pile of clothes. Dad was stark naked, standing in the running shower and Jessica stood just outside the shower using a floor mop to clean him off. Joe was yelling and demanding that she "STOP."

Jimmy finally regained his composure enough to ask Jessica if she needed any help. She just yelled back, "NO!" Jimmy said he slowly backed out of the bedroom and into the hallway where he just stood there, not knowing whether to laugh or cry.

This was a fine thing for a 20-year-old to do! Jimmy said the picture of Jessica "mopping" her naked grandfather in the shower is a sight he will never forget!

Remember to find a good thing about your day and focus on it. Be an angel. Perform random acts of kindness.

March 1, 2004

Well, I think we may have reached is a turning point with Joe and his disease. Yesterday, Jimmy said that Joe had an accident on the carpet in his bedroom. Jimmy put Joe in the bathtub to clean him up. When Joe was out and drying himself off, he fell backwards into the bathtub and his head hit the wall. Joe was just lying there looking up at him. Jimmy got him out and dried him and put a robe on him. I came home from work and dressed him. When I went upstairs to take a nap, an hour and a half later, Joe threw up all over himself.

Since his accident in the bathtub, we've noticed several big differences. He has the hiccups and can't seem to stop. He's not drinking his coffee. He just sits there at breakfast. The kids put him to bed for me last night. When I got him up this morning he threw up again.

He didn't seem to understand, now, when I'm trying to bathe him. He won't try to dry himself, as he usually does. He refused to brush his teeth and kept biting the toothbrush when I tried to do this for him. He was mad and didn't want the toothbrush in his mouth.

I took his vitals and noted that his blood pressure was low and his pulse was higher than usual. He refused to dress himself and failed to ask for his shoes. When I gave him his shoes he seemed uninterested in putting them on. This is real unusual for Joe. He always insists on having his shoes and complains constantly until he has them on.

He only had a couple bites of breakfast and maybe a cup and a half of coffee. He has always loved breakfast and his coffee. He still has the hiccups, but his vitals are normal now. He still won't really eat or drink and can't concentrate on anything I say.

I know the disease is making him worse and I know the day will come when he goes into the 3rd, and last, stage of Alzheimers. I fear my shopping days with him are now over. He just loves walking in the grocery stores, leaning on the grocery cart. He's so slow now that it takes forever to shop with him.

It seems like he can hardly walk now and this happened from just a few days ago.

March 3, 2004

Dad still doesn't seem to have an appetite. He's very listless and not walking around or responding as he normally does, so I took him to the Emergency Room at the hospital. Of course they ran all kinds of tests and then admitted him into the hospital. He has pneumonia.

They also gave him a swallowing test and found that clear liquids are going into his trachea. This was the cause of his pneumonia. It was a weird day. When I went to the hospital and spoke to the person who gave him the swallowing test, she said that Dad responded very well for her. He followed commands correctly and can eat pretty well, even though he's missing his back teeth. She said I would have to thicken up the clear liquids like coffee, pop or water.

When I left, I asked the nurses to have the doctor call me and tell me the results of the tests. When the doctor called he told me that he couldn't wake Joe up. He said that he was unresponsive, could no longer eat and needed to have a feeding tube put in. He then informed me that I'll need to put Dad in a nursing home and that he may very well not make it through the night.

Of course I had to argue with him. I said I was just there a few hours ago and Dad was perfectly responsive. I said I'd spoken with the lady who administered the swallowing test and that she'd told me that Dad could certainly eat food; that he was having a problem with clear liquids only.

Well, I went back to the hospital fearing the worst but when I got to his room, there was Dad, feisty as ever. He'd taken his clothes off and had almost crawled out of the bed. The oxygen tubing was pulled away from his nose. He was caught between the bed rails and they were the only thing keeping him from getting out of bed. I called in a nurse to help me put him back to bed. Then I called the doctor from Dad's room to report his condition. The doctor was amazed and said he'd come right away. Then he chickened out and sent a colleague.

The new doctor was very nice. He's trying to line up some hospice workers to help us out. They will get us a wheelchair, in case Dad can't walk much anymore, and will see that we have a supply of oxygen if he still needs it. They'll come to the house and help us with baths, vitals and most anything else we need. I think she said they would give us four hours respite care a week.

In any case, right now he's still in the hospital and they are still checking the lab work. I had to fight with them to let Dad *eat*. If there are no more test then why can't he eat? I talked to the nurses who told me they had to wait for "orders." I called the doctor and his nurse told the nurses on Dad's floor to change the orders to soft food.

Sometimes I think that we are just numbers and if we don't make a noise, we are forgotten. Dad keeps asking to come home but is also sleeping a lot. Hospice will bring him home by ambulance and I think Medicare pays for this. Anyway Dad is "himself" again and all is good.

March 5, 2004

Well, I had work my 24-hour shift yesterday, so I couldn't see Dad at the hospital. Jessica visited him and the nurse told her he wasn't eating. When I got off work this morning, around 9 a.m., I went by the hospital. I noticed food trays in the hall but there was no tray in Dad's room. The nurse told me that he only took two bites, so I asked for the tray back and told her that he loves to eat. I woke him up, gave him his breakfast tray back and he went to town on his food. The nurse came in and seemed very surprised. She said I must "have a way with him."

I was also complimented on his skin. They said his skin looks so good that I must really take good care of him. I shaved him, made him brush his teeth and then called the doctor who came in to see me along with the hospice nurse. I told them that Dad won't get well in the hospital, and I can't be here all the time to make sure he eats his meals. They agreed with me that he'd be better off at home.

Dad's home now and we have oxygen and a wheelchair, in case he needs them. I'm waiting for the hospice nurse to get here and remove the catheter. He seems pretty unsteady on his feet and can't walk very well. I'll try to get him to exercise his legs again, but all that stopped, of course, when he went in the hospital. It's hard to tell if this is just a result of the pneumonia and hospitalization or is a symptom of Alzheimer's.

The hospice nurse finally arrived and removed the catheter. I gave Joe a hamburger, but he could only eat half the sandwich. I'm guessing that, since he hasn't eaten much the past few days, it will take a while for his appetite to return to normal. He's complaining that his upper stomach hurts. I think this is indigestion and the hospital gave me some medicine for that.

He actually got up and started walking around, slowly. I guess I don't need anyone to teach him to walk again.

March 14, 2004

What a pretty Sunday morning. It is always so pretty here to see the sun come up over the mountains. We started our day like we usually do on Sunday mornings and went to church. We brought Dad in a wheelchair. He always sits there as though he's listening. I hold his hand when he begins to get agitated from sitting so long. I whisper "Hush" in his ear when he tells me we have to go. I remind him that we're in church. He always says he's sorry but then, a few minutes later, it starts all over again.

March, 2004, Jessica, Regina and Joe.

Today we are celebrating Regina's birthday. She will turn seventeen tomorrow. We went to an Italian restaurant for dinner. Joe was a little impatient as we waited for our food but he did enjoy his meal even though he didn't eat all of it. He was ready to leave, of course, just as soon as he finished.

It's getting hard to take him out now. I want so desperately for him not to get worse. I go back in my mind and concentrate on when we were all younger. In those days, Dad would go out with us to celebrate birthdays and laugh and joke and be the life of the party. I keep thinking that somehow I can bring that back. In reality, though, I only have photos and memories that live on. Remember that life is short. Tell someone today that you love them.

March 16, 2004

I've seen some major changes in Dad in the past few weeks. He doesn't brush his teeth anymore; he will brush his face, instead. He does not put on his socks anymore—he doesn't seem to know *what* they are. He's also a little more agitated than usual. This could be because I only give him one Risperdal a day instead of two. The Hospice Nurse has him on sleeping pills at bedtime. I restrain him at night so he won't get up, fall and hurt himself. He does get winded much faster than he use to. Yet, he still walks up and down the hall to the front door and back.

He wants to go out, but when I take him out in his wheelchair for a walk, we are hardly a couple of doors away when, suddenly, he's in a hurry to get back home. I'll take him on a walk anyway and he prays the whole time we're gone and looks everywhere for our house. It's hard to take him to a restaurant now because he can't sit and wait for the food. As soon as he eats, he wants to leave. Hospice is coming over twice a week to bathe Joe while I'm at work. He's still on oxygen but doesn't seem to need it very often.

He's now having regular bowel movements but no longer seems to know it so I have to keep checking him so he won't get a rash. He garbles now instead of talks. It's sad but interesting to see how this disease works in small ways over time.

Remember never to put off tomorrow what you can say and do today.

April 20, 2004

It's been well over a month since Dad was hospitalized and he's doing much better now. We don't need to restrain him at night and he's walking around the house like he used to. His mental confusion is increasing, however, as the disease progresses. Sometimes he almost drives me nuts by repeating the same sentence over and over again. Sometimes he'll do this for an hour or more, without stopping.

He doesn't like using the oxygen so we've restricted it to only a couple of hours a day. If he's tired and sitting still, I'll try to get him to put it on because, as a rule, he'll fall asleep and not notice it. If he's wide awake, however, he watches for me to leave the room or get distracted and then—off goes the oxygen. He still walks from the living room to the front door and back. Most of the time he locks the door (without knowing it), but if he finds he can open it, he walks out and then comes right back in.

He doesn't answer questions anymore. It's very hard to get his attention now. His mind will be set on something or he'll be repeating a phrase and simply can't see or hear you, so he doesn't answer. The only thing he can still do is put on his pants, eat, and walk the halls.

He doesn't like to be shaved anymore. He complains the whole time and I really don't think he knows what I'm doing. He tries to get me to put his slacks on him. I do everything else now and I know that pretty soon he won't even be able to do that so I make him do it.

He still pleads with me to take him somewhere—anywhere. So I put him in the wheelchair and take him out for a walk. At first he seems very happy, but after we pass a couple houses, he begins to complain. He can still be pretty ugly at times.

Hospice is still coming over twice a week to bathe him and once a week for vitals.

May 30, 2004

This Sunday morning Dad really wasn't himself. He couldn't seem to do anything. He couldn't get out of bed and I had to walk him to the bathroom and pick his legs up and put him in the tub. He couldn't stand up in the tub and Jimmy had to help me get him out.

Easter, 2004, in Arizona, Left to right: Marie, Jimmy, Adias, Regina, Joe (seated), Zack (Jessica's fiancé) and Jessica.

I shaved him while he was sitting on his bed instead of in his usual position, standing by the bathroom sink. The most unusual behavior of all was that he *never* complained.

After I got him dressed, I had to stand him up and walk him to the living room. Jimmy gave him his coffee and toast but it seemed like he couldn't hold the cup.

We took him to church, but we had to take him in the wheelchair because he couldn't seem to stand or walk. After church, Jessica made Grandpa some soup. When I walked him to the kitchen table, he didn't want to eat and didn't seem to know how to hold the spoon. I fed him the soup with lots of crackers to thicken it and he spit it back at me a couple of times.

He also can't seem not to hold a glass of pop. He really loves his pop, so this is a very bad sign. We're wondering if maybe he had another stroke.

June 7, 2004

New findings on Dad include the fact that for the past week he has not urinated during the day. He doesn't ask to go to the bathroom anymore. He urinates only at night when he sleeps. He doesn't walk around anymore and can't seem to get up out of bed or his chair. When he does get up he either walks very slowly using baby steps or I hold his hands and pull him around.

He doesn't make sense anymore when he talks. He can't seem to hold a fork, spoon or his glass very well. He seems to drink less and less and that is unusual since he loves coffee and pop. I must give him his cups half-full now because he keeps spilling them.

His pores smell like urine. I'm not sure if this means he is going through organ death. His pupils seem more constricted. He is losing weight since he's not eating.

His skin still looks good but I'm afraid that he'll be bed-bound soon and then I'll have to watch for bedsores.

He did have diarrhea the other day. I was at work and poor Gina was taking care of him. I told her she was going to have to clean him up. We fought about it but she finally took care of Grandpa and cleaned him up. When I called her back she was crying. This is a hard thing for a 17-year-old girl to do. Now he's getting a rash and I'll need to put ointment on him.

June 8, 2004

Well things have taken a turn for the worst. It started last night when we came home from our walk and Dad ate an ice cream cone. Suddenly he just slumped over and didn't move a muscle. As we got him ready for bed, Gina said that he was like a rag doll. He couldn't even help us by standing up. We managed to undress him with one of us holding him up and the other one undressing and dressing him. We laid him in bed and that is how I found him this morning. It appears that he threw up some last night. He also had the hiccups.

This morning he barely responded to me. I got him on the toilet and that is where I bathed him, undressed him and dressed him, brushed his teeth and shaved him. I could not get him to walk to the living room so Jimmy had to hold him while I got his wheelchair.

He doesn't respond to even simple commands like, "Squeeze my hands." I can't get him to eat or drink. He didn't even have a full cup of coffee. He spit his cereal out at me and told me, "NO" when I tried to give him some scrambled eggs.

He's running a temperature of 102.7. I finally got him to eat two spoons of applesauce to which I added some crushed non-aspirin. He still won't eat or drink. We are discussing the possibility of using a feeding tube but we're very unsure about what to do.

We think that we should let him die naturally, yet we don't want to starve him. I talked to the hospice nurse about this. She said that if it's his time to go, then we couldn't change that even with a feeding tube. Without drinking water, of course, his body can only last so long. She seemed to think that he would probably get pneumonia again and could die from that.

In any case, the hospice nurse will be here tomorrow and help us with these decisions.

Please pray for Jimmy, this is real hard for him. Thank you for all your prayers.

June 10, 2004

It is a little harder than I thought it would be to watch Dad die. He's been running a high fever for a couple of days now. His fever seems to be down now and he just sleeps. He doesn't eat or drink—just sleeps. We were given Lorazepam (a sedative) and morphine sublingual (absorbed under the tongue) and ASA (aspirin)to be administered in suppositories.

Now we are waiting for the hospital bed and the hospice aide to arrive and help get him out of his chair where he's been for the last couple of days. When we get him into bed, then I can wash and change him. Jimmy tried to help me get him up but Dad started shaking so bad that it scared Jimmy away. I'm letting him stay there till Gary, the hospice aide, gets here. Dad's getting that death smell. I swab his mouth and try to keep it moist.

I imagine it is just days now.

Gary, the hospice nurse, finally arrived and we just finished with Dad. Gary is such a good man. He's Italian and Irish. He helped me get Dad to his bed. This was hard for

Jimmy to watch as Dad would shake his arms, legs and entire body very fast but without a beat. We managed to get him into his bed with Jimmy's help but that was all Jim could stand.

Gary washed Joe as I helped him. I changed the linens. I noticed some problems which developed during the two days he sat in his chair. His skin is already starting to break down and we found some bedsores on his foot and buttocks. I'll have to be careful and keep turning him and washing to prevent these.

Joe is sleeping peacefully while we await the arrival of his hospital bed. We're keeping his mouth moist and the oxygen on him. There's not much else we can do but just try to keep him comfortable as his time draws near.

Thank you for all your prayers. It is hard to watch a loved one die. But I am so glad that he is here with us and not in a nursing home.

June 11, 2004

These days are getting harder and harder. I spent most of the morning at work, crying as I cleaned out my ambulance. I thought it would be easier when he was going through the process of dying. I've known all along that this day would come. But I think that nothing can really prepare you for the death of a loved one.

I was with my sister when she died. We held her hand and talked to her while she took her last breath. So why is this so hard? I walk into his bedroom and see this 78-year-old man. He's just lying there. He has no expression, no movement. He is totally lifeless. His skin feels hot, so I put in another supposi-tory of aspirin to try to cool down his body. I give him mor-phine to help relax him. When I move him from side to side he starts to shake and his eyes open, but he cannot focus. His pupils are small and constricted.

I gave him a bath today. He woke up for a moment, shak-ing and making sounds. He's like a rag doll. He just lies there and lets me roll him around. I would like to know what he is thinking or even *if* he is thinking. What is he dreaming about?

Knowing that he is dying is one thing, but watching him die and going so slowly is torture. I'm finding it hard to con-centrate or focus on anything. I can't seem to get anything done. Calling the funeral home and insurance company is a hard job also. I had no idea what all it consists of *to die.*

Poor Jimmy is trying to study for school through all this. He's always getting mad at himself if he can't remember some-thing. How hard this must be for him.

June 12, 2004

It's hard to believe, but Dad made it through another night. Gary, our hospice aide, came over and washed and shaved Dad this morning. Joe seems pretty comfortable but has turned again for the worst. He is breathing 40 times a minute making a loud gasp with each breath. His fingernails and knees and lips are showing a tinge of blue. He's sweating profusely and running a temperature of 103.

I gave him another suppository of aspirin and more Lorazapam and morphine.

June 13, 2004

The night is long as I sit here on my father-in-law's bed watching him die. His fingers are turning white and I hear the crackles from his chest each time he takes a breath. Foam is coming from the corners of his mouth. His pulse is racing as his body fights to breathe but he is asleep through all this. Peacefully asleep.

I reflect on the man he was, so full of life, so kind and generous. I think about how often he helped me and my children. I'm not sure that giving him even these two years can begin to repay his kindness. It is so terrifying to see him die yet so comforting to know he will be in a better place soon. Heaven.

Got up at 3:00 a.m., and Dad is still breathing through his mouth. I can feel a pretty good pulse in his wrist. His arms are very cold. I gave him some more morphine and laid next to him. I laid my hand on his chest and told him it was time to "Go home." I gave him a kiss and went back to bed.

This morning I got up around 8:00 a.m., and noticed that Dad was breathing fast, almost 32 times a minute. I can hear some gurgling and his body feels very warm. I gave him his medicine.

I think the hardest part now is the wait. Even though I saw him just before this phase, unable to talk, eat, hold anything, urinate, or walk, I can't help wondering, "Am I killing him?"

His heart is still beating strong while the rest of him is dying. His mind is gone now and we watched him go through so many, so many stages of this disease. Now that his death could come at any time, we still wonder, "Should we put a feeding tube in him? Should we keep him hooked up to IV's? Should we constantly turn his body to keep from bed sores?"

What kind of quality of life is that for him? His heart wants to go on, yet his mouth opens and gasps for air with each breath. And we feel so helpless.

We wonder, "Is he suffering?" He lies there, completely lifeless. All we can hear or see is the gasping of air with each breath. It is torture to watch this and we begin to wish that the heavenly father would just take him home.

Well, today is the day that Joe went to heaven to be with Jesus. He left us at about 12:15 p.m., this Sunday afternoon. I am sure that his wife and his Mom and Dad and other relatives are waiting for him.

He made it through the night, breathing with his mouth open and abdominal muscles working. His nail beds were blue and his arms were cold. Still, I could feel a pulse in his wrist.

Yet this morning his arms were warm. But I noticed that his body was mottled with colors of purple and pink. His ears were a dark blue. His diaper was wet. When I changed him and washed his body, I could see all the places that the color blue was appearing. Then, as I finished and got him dressed again, he started gulping.

Suddenly, I could not feel a pulse in his wrist anymore. I called to Jimmy and Gina ran in after him. I told them that he didn't have long now. Jimmy and I sat on either side of him, rubbing his arms and his head, telling him that we loved him and what a great man he was. Gina sat in the corner, just watching us. Then he finally stopped breathing.

The hardest part is the wait.

We watched him try to breathe and waited for the inevitable.

Sadly now, this part of our life is over, but we know that a new adventure will come again. I think I've forgotten, these past two weeks, what it is like to smile. But life goes on.

Sometimes I wish everything could just stop for a minute and let me catch my breath. Then I could start up again.

Remember life is short. Don't take it for granted. Tell someone you love them. Do an act of kindness. And always pray.

Helpful Resources

Gruetcher, Howard. *Alzheimer's A Caregivers Guide and Sourcebook*. John Wiley & Son's, 2001.

Kuhn, David. *Alzheimer's Early Stages*. Hunter House, 2003.

Larken, Marilynn. *When Someone You Love Has Alzheimer's*, Dell Publishing,1995.

Marcell, Jacqueline. *Elder Rage or, take My Father ... Please! How to Survive, Caring for Aging Parents*. Impressive Press, 2000

Parrent, Joanne. *Courage to Care: A Caregiver's Guide Through each Stage of Alzheimer's*. Alpha, 2001.

Shenk, David. *The Forgetting: Alzheimer's: Portrait Of An Epidemic*. First Anchor Paper Edition, 2003

Strauss, Claudia. *Talking to Alzheimer's*, New Harbinger Publications, 2002.

AlzheimersSupport.com
Includes: Information, understanding, treatment, drug news, resources, support groups, message boards, chat room, caregiver's corner.

Alzfdn.org
Alzheimer's Foundation of America, "Together for Care ... In Addition to Cure." This Foundation is dedicated to education and care to individuals and their families.

Alzheimers.org
Alzheimer's Disease Education and Referral Center. Includes: general information, causes, symptoms, diagnosis, treatment and highlights of new publications.

General Symptoms of Alzheimer's Disease

The three stages of Alzheimer's are:

Stage 1
    gradual short-term memory loss
    losing and hiding things
    wandering
    experiences emotional changes
    displays odd and inappropriate behavior
    tends to be suspicious and/or accusing

Stage 2
    Severe memory loss
    difficulty speaking
    difficulty communicating
    difficulty understanding
    restlessness
    easily agitated
    bad hygiene practices
    tendency to wander and/or get lost
    "sun-downing"
    sleep disturbances
    behaving childishly
    hallucinating
    resents caregivers
    displays anger
    clinging behavior

Stage 3
    severe speech impairment
    displays very little awareness of surroundings
    extreme loss of mental functions
    refuses to eat
    displays complete dependency
    incontinence
    inability to perform most activities

READER'S NOTES

_____

_____

_____

_____

_____

_____

_____

_____

_____

_____

_____

_____

CPSIA information can be obtained at www.ICGtesting.com
Printed in the USA
LVOW100707250912

300209LV00005B/16/A